MW01596226

Stormie's Joy

When Animals Heal Our Hearts

Stormie Conway

bhc press™

Livonia, Michigan

The events described in this book are true. However, some names, locations, and breeds of dogs have been changed to protect those who prefer their identities to remain anonymous.

Editor: Sara Haskins

STORMIE'S JOY

Copyright © 2019 Stormie Conway

All rights reserved. No part of this publication may be reproduced, distributed, or transmitted in any form or by any means, including photocopying, recording, or other electronic or mechanical methods, without the prior written permission of the publisher, except in the case of brief quotations embodied in critical reviews and certain other noncommercial uses permitted by copyright law. For permission requests, please write to the publisher.

Published by BHC Press

Library of Congress Control Number: 2018959724

ISBN Numbers:
978-1-64397-015-8 (Hardcover)
978-1-948540-52-0 (Softcover)
978-1-948540-53-7 (Ebook)

For information, write:
BHC Press
885 Penniman #5505
Plymouth, MI 48170

Visit the publisher:
www.bhcpress.com

For Vinny, the man in my life,
for standing by me day in and day out
while I hammered out my thoughts or griped
about having no thoughts at all.

Acknowledgments

First to the glory of God from whom all blessings flow, including His abundant grace without which I would be unable to construct a coherent sentence. A heartfelt thank you to all my friends who urged me on during those times when I thought I'd hit one too many brick walls. I thank Sue who provided the gentle and wise voice of reason on those several occasions when I found it difficult to couch my words in a way that would neither create hard feelings on the part of those about whom I wrote nor compromise my stories. My gratitude also to Teri and Stephen for their generosity in loaning me their laptop so I didn't have to go weeks without writing while I cared for animals where I had no computer at my disposal. Finally, this work is the direct result of Mike Kewer's admonition, "You should write a book." His words excited me, fueled me, and drove me to begin and complete this project. Thank you, Mike.

Herein follow the stories of my encounters and interaction with the animals, as well as glimpses into my past that shaped me into the impetuous, sometimes depressed, but always blessed and near-normal person I am today. I hope you enjoy reading them as much as I enjoyed sharing them.

"Not everything in life
is a good poop.
Neutralize the would-be
bad stuff by greeting
every person, animal,
and experience with an
open and joyful heart.
Even scary thunder yields
in the face of optimism."

~ Buddy ~

Stormie's Joy

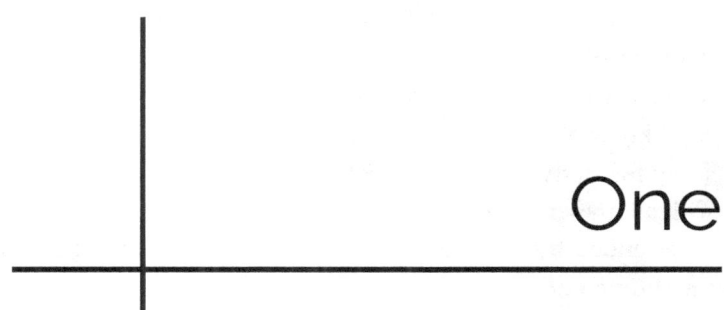

One

Truth: bugs scare the pants off me, in particular, those bugs larger than a small pea and that skitter around faster than I can blink.

Enter Baxter, a young black Lab mix with a huge heart and more loose screws than the Cadbury bunny has marshmallow eggs. When I met Baxter, he lived in a beautiful New Jersey lake community house with Bea, a sweet, long-haired Dachshund, and Betty, a paranoid (not without cause) cat. Also, a colony of cave crickets that plotted against me. You scoff, but I kid you not! Just when I'd think it was safe to relax my vigilance, I'd see one lurking in the shadows of a potted plant or maybe one creeping out from behind the bathroom sink. *Oy!* Between Baxter and Bea chasing Betty around the house and the crickets terrorizing me at every turn, the Zen-like therapy I sought on the woods-ensconced deck often dissolved into frenzied chaos.

But Baxter with his 40 pounds of kinetic energy, insatiable demand for attention, and loopy personality made for laugh-filled assignments which were therapeutic in and of themselves. Once was a time when, had anyone asked me, I'd have described Baxter in anthropomorphic terms as a dog into himself, oblivious of everything around him except for that which directly impacted his world. How wrong I would have been in that assessment!

I remember one raucous chase scene that ended with Betty fleeing to the basement from the dogs who could not fit through the "cat door" leading down the stairs. The cave crickets hung out in force in the basement, so I avoided that part of the house as much as possible. But I knew of sliding doors to the outside world down there, and I felt sorry for Betty who sought escape from the in-house craziness. So, with all my senses on high alert for any sign of those infernal crickets, I descended the basement stairs. *Whew!* No crickets. Betty stood by the sliding doors, and I hurried over to let her out.

And then I saw it! The plotting cave crickets had called out their big guns. On the white curtain, just inches from the door handle, sat a black spider the likes of which I'd never seen in my life. With a body larger than a quarter and its curved legs close to an inch in length, the creature looked like something out of a Stephen King novel. I froze. I heard the sound of my heart jackhammering in my chest, or maybe it was the silence of my heart not beating at all.

As I stood there facing off with that frightful candidate for the lead role in Arachnophobia 117, Baxter materialized beside me. (I must have left the upstairs door open so I could make a quick getaway from a sniper cricket if necessary.) Baxter waited beside me, not chasing Betty, but looking up at me as if to say, "It's okay, Stormie. I'm here. I'll protect you." And somehow, with him there, I rediscovered the muscles in my legs and inched toward the door. Baxter inched with me. Betty waited by the door. The menacing spider crouched on the curtain and was decent enough not to move as I reached my hand forward to push the curtain aside ever so gently and ever so slowly. And it did not move when I slid the door open for Betty and then reclosed it letting the curtain fall back into place.

I backed away from the door, and Baxter, sensing the crisis had passed, bolted up the stairs. By the time I reached the top of the stairs, Baxter had reverted to his normal ebullient self and bounced around like a cork in a wind-whipped ocean when he saw me heading for his bag of bacon treats. He seemed to have no memory of his recent heroics, or perhaps he just accepted the role of protecting common humans from creatures that go bump in the night as part and parcel of his job.

To this day, I don't know why or how Baxter suppressed his natural exuberance and egocentric mentality long enough to "rescue" me. Maybe, like I've read in so many stories about dogs, he heard the changes in my heartbeat, and when push came to inevitable shove, he responded to his canine legendary instinct to protect.

Baxter and his family moved to Maryland a few years later—to the shores of another lake. Crickets and spiders may live there, too. But if Baxter is on duty, the perimeter is secure, and all his family safe.

How I came to know Baxter and company is a story in and of itself. When the price of gas soared through the roof in the mid-2000s, I joined the masses who refused to pay $4.00 a gallon and opted for commuting to work by train. I overheard one chatty passenger who waited for the morning train with us express a need for a pet sitter. I hadn't done a lot of pet sitting at the time, much less begun a business, but I had toyed with the idea of leaving the corporate rat race and caring for animals full time. So, while not the most gregarious of individuals, I summoned all my courage, sat across from the woman when we boarded the train, and squeaked, "I hear you need someone to care for your animals. I'll do it." Her immediate response, "You will?" Then began a conversation in which Viki told me that she and her husband, George, planned to attend the New Orleans Jazz festival in a couple of months and needed someone to care for their two dogs, a Dachshund (Bea), an old Golden Retriever (Bogey), and a cat (Betty). We scheduled a meet and greet, during which George told me he would pay me $50 a day to care for their animals. I had had no idea how much to charge, and George's offer sounded more than fair to me for the opportunity to love three animals. I accepted the assignment.

This would be my first "paid" assignment from which others would develop, and my eventual business, "Stormie's Joy," would emerge.

Viki and George called upon me to pet sit several times, and then I received the sad news that Bogey had been put to sleep. They had since acquired a black Lab puppy, Baxter. Baxter was frightened to death of me when I arrived to care for him the first time at his by then empty-of-humans house. He hid behind the drapes shaking and quaking, and when I attempted to coax him out, he dashed past me and up the stairs to take root under Viki and George's bed. Nothing I did could entice him to leave his safe place, and when I put a little peanut butter on the tip of a broomstick and slid it under the bed in hopes of convincing him that I was a friend, he shocked me by attacking it and leaving teeth marks in the wood. At one point, he even defecated under the bed. This dog was terrified.

I formulated a plan. I would take Bea for a walk (the panacea for almost all dysfunctional behaviors) and call my friend, Alice, to act as my partner in crime. Baxter might follow us out, in which case, Alice could maybe get a leash on him. It was a cinch he wouldn't let me do it. Sure enough, as Alice, Bea and I left the house leaving the front door wide open, Baxter slunk out behind us and allowed Alice to leash him while eyeing me with suspicion, giving every indication that I was a must to avoid. The four of us continued our walk, during which Baxter allowed me to hold his leash and pet him without him tucking his tail too far between his legs. By the time we returned home, Baxter appeared to have forgotten whatever it was that had freaked him out about me and accepted a bacon treat from my hand.

My relationship with Baxter continued to improve after the initial hiccup to the point that he and Bea both slept on the bed with me from that first night on. And after a couple of days, when we walked through the woods across the street from his house, I could unleash him and watch him bound off through the trees and up and over the rocks. He never went far, always stayed within sight of me, and always came to me when I whistled for him. In short, he was a happy dog who loved life for what it was, and I was sad when he, Bea and Betty and their humans moved to Maryland.

About creepy crawlies, I remember a time while I cared for two cats and two dogs in Montville. Once, after completing my normal morning routine, I emerged from the downstairs guestroom into the large family room to see Fred and Gene, the two cats, fascinated by something on the carpet. Of course, I had to look and saw with a sinking heart a large black spider (not of the same caliber as the one Baxter and I had taken on, but larger than the normal little gray ones that hang out in corners presenting a danger to no one). I fought my knee-jerk reaction to freeze on the spot. Instead, after watching Fred and Gene torment the spider, my natural aversion to seeing any living creature suffer trumped my trembling, and I began to think about how to release the spider to the outdoors. The first step involved containment and protection from two very intrigued cats. One of the cocktail glasses on a nearby table looked like a perfect and safe means to accomplish step one, so marshaling every ounce of courage I had, I very carefully and very slowly upended a glass over the spider. Next, I located a sheet of paper with a CD attached to it in Debbie's dance studio and slid the whole thing under the glass and under the spider. And then I carried the entire rig out through the garage, lifted the glass from the paper, and nudged the spider into the bushes. Spent the rest of the day feeling super accomplished and puffed up. I mean, I had vanquished the fearsome beastie lurking outside my bedroom door and had called for help from no one. Had I been at home when I saw it, and had I handled the situation with the same aplomb, I would have indulged in a well-deserved glass of Chocolate Amore sooner, rather than later, in the day.

But my complacency was short lived. On the last day of my assignment while in the middle of packing, I saw another one of those spiders. Before I could catch my breath and reconstruct the spider-removal device that had worked so well a few days earlier, the creature had crawled under a sofa, not to be seen by me again that day. The sight of the second spider unnerved me more than the first. One lone menacing spider scared me. The thought of two or more such creatures downright petrified me—to the point that I included in my assignment summation to Debbie and Phil a request that they hire an exterminator. I just didn't see myself cohabitating with a clutter of spiders.

Two

I met the handsome tuba-playing aficionado, Roger, in September 1980 when we were both working toward our BS in Psychology and happened to enroll in the same night class, "Theories of Personality." While we never dated per se, we developed a close friendship, engaged in long philosophical discussions, rode our bicycles together, and threw a football around. Well, he threw a football; I tried to catch it and attempted to throw it back. Never could get the hang of getting the ball to spiral.

I met Steve on a cold Mischief Night in 1981 after merging my new (to me) 200 cc Honda Twinstar into rush-hour traffic. Steve, too, was on a motorcycle—an adult-sized motorcycle—and I just tucked in behind him and hoped he wasn't laughing too hard at the motorized roller skate following in his wake. A short while later, he pulled over to the side of the road and motioned for me to do the same. I did so, expecting him to criticize me for something stupid or dangerous I had done while behind him, or maybe to express annoyance that an obvious greenhorn had slid in behind him. Instead, what followed was a short conversation, an exchange of telephone numbers, and the first serious and meaningful romantic relationship of my life.

With the addition of Steve into my life, my relationship with Roger shifted. A trio of sorts took shape, and it worked well. We would sometimes ride our motorcycles together or hang out over dinner. One time, Steve and Roger engaged in a kamikaze racquetball match incorporating a super ball (one of those hard, crazy, high-bouncing balls) and motorcycle helmets to protect against further damage to their brains. Our times together were somewhat superficial but lots of fun.

Four years happened in a blink during which time, Roger moved away to parts unknown, and Steve and I broke up but remained friends. Sometime later, Steve married and moved to Virginia with his family, two master's degrees and a doctorate to teach college students about environmental protection.

Two years ago in 2016, I found Roger again (after maybe thirty years) through the miracle of Facebook. He had married and lived with his family in Michigan where they devoted large slices of their lives to rescuing greyhounds and cats. Kudos to Roger and his wife, Denise! We chatted a bit online, and one day, my cell phone rang indicating a number I didn't recognize. I make it a practice to not answer such numbers, because I hate telemarketing and robocalls. But this time, a little voice told me to answer the call. It was Roger, and we talked for almost four hours doing our best to cram decades past into our conversation until our phone batteries died. One of the best four hours I'd spent in a long time.

Roger and I continued to pop into each other's lives now and again through Facebook. Sometimes he'd forward recordings of concerts to me in which he'd performed with his tuba. Phenomenal things, those concerts.

One day, I received a text from Roger saying he and his wife had been invited to Scotland for his best friend's wedding and asking if I would I be willing to drive to Michigan to care for his animals. He offered generous compensation, and I'd have agreed to his terms in a heartbeat had I not been committed to another client during the time he needed me. *Sigh!* How cool it would have been to see Roger again and to meet Denise. And how wonderful it would have been for me to have had the chance to play with greyhounds for the first time.

Later, I couldn't help laughing to myself when thinking I'd had the chance to take my small business national. But life throws all kinds of opportunities and curve balls at us. Who knows? One day, the universe may toss a high fly in my direction, and I'll catch it and find myself en route to Michigan embarking on a brand-new adventure and creating future glory days of my own—like those in Bruce Springsteen's song!

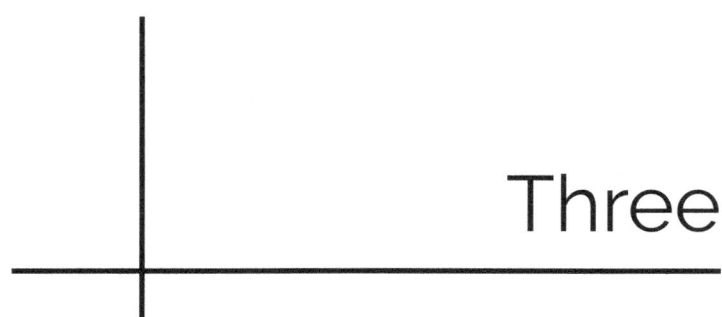

Three

Steve and I hit it off at light speed after our initial meeting on mischief night. He could talk about anything, and our conversations challenged me to think, a quality I find very sexy. Sometimes in response to my questions, Steve would spiel on about Einstein's theory of relativity while I sat there mesmerized without understanding a word of what he said but fascinated by the concept. My eyes glazed over a lot, and my mind stretched when listening to Steve talk, never pompous or arrogant in what he said. Just so far over my head.

He invited me to spend our first Thanksgiving together with his brother Dick and family in Virginia. Some hesitation on my part. Feared I would be a boring traveling companion. But Steve would have none of it, and away we went. And a happy Thanksgiving it was.

LOVE AT FIRST SIGHT

While cruising around Virginia on Thanksgiving Saturday and checking out some beautiful countryside, Steve and I saw a billboard advertising Evergreen Arabians. I had had it in mind for a while to buy a Morgan, but "Let's go see the Arabians." So, ignoring the billboard's specification, "By Appointment Only," we drove out through horse country to the farm in Leesburg, Virginia and rang the doorbell.

The owners whose names I don't remember were gracious beyond words to the two of us and showed us around their sprawling idyllic estate, the spotless airy barn, and paddock after paddock of beautiful dappled yearlings, which were worlds beyond my range of expertise. No way was I in the market for a horse that needed to be trained from square one, even if I could afford such an animal. But we "oohed" and "ahhed" over the yearlings, thanked the couple for their time, and prepared to leave.

And, then, on the far side of another paddock, I saw a lone beautiful chestnut-colored horse that looked older than the yearlings. I

Flame

stopped, pointed to the horse, and asked, "What about that one?"

I was told he was a four-year old gelding who was green broke and one of the sweetest horses they had. His name was Evergreen Flame, and he was for sale. We lured Flame over to the fence where we stood with handfuls of sweet feed. I fell in love. Not only was he a gorgeous copper color and as sweet as described, but he was small at 14'2"—a large pony. Perfect for pint-sized me.

In response to my request to ride him, a saddle and bridle materialized. I watched as Flame offered no resistance to either piece of equipment, and with a leg up, I was off. Yes, he was green broke and a bit of a handful for a relative novice like myself, but his gait was the smoothest I'd ever experienced. And unlike many horses, he didn't take advantage of my meager riding ability. We formed some kind of immediate and intangible bond, and I think he figured we could teach each other and learn together.

I dismounted Flame and never surer of anything in my life than I wanted that horse, I handed over a deposit check for the owners to hold him and continue working with him while I returned to New Jersey to come up with the several thousand dollars balance.

Steve and I stopped at a diner on our way home from Virginia, and while I bit into my hamburger, Steve spoke words I will never forget. "I want you to be happy, and I will do whatever it takes to make you happy. If you ever need any money for anything like to buy your Flame, I want you to come to me. Will you do that? Will you do that for me?" I think my heart may have burst at his words. Not with a giddy kind of love and happiness but a feeling of calm assurance that all was right with the world. I was young and healthy, had a wonderful man who loved me, a well-paying and secure (if not the most satisfying) job, and I was about to become a first-time horse owner, something that had been on my wish list from as far back as I could remember.

PAPERWORK

So, how to finance Flame? I didn't want to take Steve up on his offer if I could help it. Well, I had a motorcycle. Maybe, just maybe…

I drove to the bank after work the following Monday. With my credit in good standing and the pink slip to my motorcycle as collateral, would the people who doled out money be willing to front me a few thousand dollars so I could buy a horse? The Stormie-sympathetic and horse-loving gods of the universe smiled upon me, and the bank granted my loan. Yes! Scary but necessary paperwork was signed, and a check was forwarded to Evergreen Arabians with a letter asking them to hold off transporting Flame to New Jersey until I found a place for him to live.

THE INTERVIEW

I wanted the perfect set-up for Flame. After checking out several local stables and finding not one that satisfied all my criteria of being well maintained with stalls that opened to the outside, having plenty of paddock room, housing healthy-looking horses, and being within my price range, discouragement hit hard. Fate had been toying with me; I was never meant to have Flame or any horse yet.

But one day at work, a coworker and horse owner told me about a woman, Mrs. A., who ran a stable that had an excellent reputation. Sue gave me the woman's telephone number saying she didn't know Mrs. A. well but did know her daughter, Jessie.

More nervous than I'd been for any job interview, I called Mrs. A. as soon as I returned home from work and explained my situation. I mentioned Sue's name, and Mrs. A. who had sounded reluctant about taking in another horse, changed her attitude and invited me over to the house so we could meet. Her address was less than ten minutes from where I lived. Kismet!

I drove over to meet Mrs. A. the following day at the appointed time and was delighted with what I saw as I drove up the long driveway: several large fenced-in paddocks, a well-kept outdoor ring, and a barn with stall doors that allowed the horses plenty of ventilation and the ability to face outside. Mrs. A. was a love and emphasized that the horses received the best of everything, including Timothy hay, high-grade sweet feed and oats, and pastures that were limed to yield full lush grass. No expense was spared in the care of the horses. She considered all the horses, not just her own, her babies. A reliable farrier visited on a regular basis to care for the horses' feet. Jessie could continue to work with Flame and give me lessons if I wanted. And several people who boarded their horses at her stable often rode out on the miles of fields and wooded trails around the property. I'd be welcome to join them. Sounded like everything I'd been looking for! I opted for rough board meaning Flame would be fed and turned out to graze and play every day, but I would be responsible for cleaning his stall. I could do that. No problem.

But I suffer from frequent cluster headaches that often send me to the mat with cold compresses, medication, total quiet, and sleep. Mrs. A. assured me that those days when a headache prohibited my caring for Flame, a phone call from Steve or me would set things in motion for the staff to feed him and maintain his stall. I need never worry about Flame's well-being.

WELCOME HOME

All that remained was for Flame to undergo and pass a Coggins test for equine infectious and incurable anemia before being transported to New Jersey. I called Evergreen Arabians, told them the good news, and asked them to see to the Coggins test and arrange for Flame's transport. All systems were go! Flame passed his Coggins test with flying colors and would travel in a jumbo trailer with two Thoroughbreds that were headed for a track. He would be at the rear of the trailer away from the two larger horses. Race horses could be bullies.

On the appointed evening of Flame's arrival, Mrs. A. and Terry (one of the stable staff) waited outside with Steve and me in a cold, wind-driven, drenching January rain. There may have been thunder and lightning, too; I don't remember. But the hour grew later, the night grew darker, and the weather did not improve. At last, the huge trailer carrying my horse arrived. It turned into the driveway, its headlights paled by the mist, and lumbered up the driveway without making any discernible sound over the heavy rain. The scene reminded me of the spectral 18-wheeler, Phantom 309 of country music fame. Eerie.

When stopped near where we all waited, the driver climbed out, dropped the side ramp to the trailer, and moved inside to retrieve Flame. A few minutes later, backlit by the bright light in the trailer, I saw my sweet gentle horse at the head of the ramp standing in front of the stalls containing the Thoroughbreds. And I watched in dismay as Flame reared up to his full height and cut his ear on the side of the van. Until then, the only sound I could hear was that of the rain drumming on the trailer. Flame's scream of mingled fury, fright and pain pierced the night like an icy blade that reached through to my bones. This could not be the horse I'd fallen in love with when in Virginia a few months ago. Steve would tell me later that the moment when Flame appeared in the doorway and reared with a shriek, he looked and sounded like a horse from hell. I would have to agree with Steve's assessment. Although the bond between Flame and me developed and strengthened into something wonderful, I was never quite sure about the relationship between Flame and Steve.

HAPPY DAYS

Flame's stall faced the parking lot, and it didn't take him long to recognize the sound of my motorcycle, my VW Rabbit, or the sight of me and issue a welcoming nicker when he saw me. He knew I bore gifts in the forms of apples or carrots for him, both of which I had to teach him how to eat. When in Virginia, he received only sweet feed for treats.

I began each day by visiting Flame to clean his stall and maybe enjoy a short ride around the paddock. The forty-five minutes to an hour of being with my horse, talking to him and loving him, calmed and readied me for the grind at Bell Labs where I felt out of place and out of sync with most of the people. I possessed none of the requisite corporate ladder-climbing ambition, but rather endured day after day of tedium answering telephones, moving papers from pile A to pile B, and engaging in pointless political corporate games. Made a pathetic showing in the latter. But a select circle of friends made the days tolerable. Ted, Ron, Linda and Paul stimulated my thinking and eased the oppressive boredom that threatened to drive me off the nearest ledge.

Even so, I counted the minutes until 4:30 when I could trip the light fantastic out of the office and return to Flame, this time to turn him out into the paddock while I mucked his stall again. You may scoff, but I found it a true labor of love, therapeutic, cleansing and rejuvenating after eight hours of sitting at a desk in front of a computer. And when the stall was clean, I'd collect Flame, pick out his hooves, groom him until he shone like the bottom of a copper pot, and either ride him around the paddock or return him to his stall for his dinner which the staff had prepared and held back when the other horses were fed.

Much as I wanted to, I didn't take my horse out on the trails. Such excursions would be a few months down the road. Flame was still not one hundred percent steady under the saddle, and I was not one hundred percent steady in the saddle. He was more of a pet for the first month or two. I played with him by running as fast as I could back and forth on the driveway while he chased me in the adjacent paddock, tail and head held high in typical Arabian fashion, whinnying and kicking up his heels in spirited delight.

Jessie, a champion rider before she suffered terrible injuries in a car accident, worked with Flame and me until I developed confidence in my seat and trust in the horse. Flame, however, taught me more about horsemanship than any lesson I'd ever had anywhere. I think he took pleasure in pitching me out of the saddle, and I think he was happy when it became more difficult for him to do so.

One of my most treasured memories with Flame, and a turning point in our relationship, is the first day I took Flame on an extended trail ride through the affluent areas of Green Village and Harding Township with Terry and three or four other people. We trotted through woods over well-worn bridal paths and cantered across fields while I imagined all kinds of future adventures with Flame. The only difficult part of that ride occurred when we needed to walk some distance alongside the road. Terrified that Flame would bolt if a car were to pass us, I tucked my chin into my neck so I couldn't see. But Terry, who had been riding behind me, brought her horse up alongside me on the outside and walked beside me until we again turned into the woods. Thank you, Terry. Your consideration and thoughtfulness at that time meant more than I can say.

From then on, I took Flame out on trails every chance I had. We crossed roads when necessary, but I never rode him for any distance in the street when we were alone. I cherished these rides through the woods with nothing but the trees, chipmunks and deer for company, and the sound of Flame's hoof beats and occasional snorting to break the silence. He was a willing horse, obeying whatever I asked of him once he understood what it was I wanted. One thing we had not done while on our group ride was cross through water, which Flame may have done with less objection had he seen the other horses do it. When it was just him and me the first time, it took much cajoling to get him to wade through the shallowest of streams. He didn't understand water and refused to engage, snorting, crab-stepping, and backing away from it when he saw it even when I dismounted and tried to lead him into it. But when he realized that water was just another medium in which to play, he splashed through it and, to my chagrin, attempted to roll in it at least once while I was on his back. Water held the added attraction during the hot humid summers of providing escape from stinging deer flies. Eating fresh-picked apples from a local orchard was a favorite thing to do. The simple act of reaching up to pluck an apple from a tree reminded me of grade school readers in which life was beautiful and perfect.

NEW BOLTON, PENNSYLVANIA

While cleaning Flame's stall one morning during our first summer together, I found no wet spot in the sawdust. Alarms clanged inside my head. I telephoned Dr. P., a local vet whom I'd called upon in the past for Flame's routine shots. He advised me to keep Flame in his stall all day so his urine output could be monitored, and he would stop by that evening. I updated Terry on what was happening, but when I returned to clean Flame's stall after work, I again saw no wet spot.

Dr. P. arrived at dusk. He examined Flame and noticed a summer sore (warm larvae deposits) on the tip of his penis that prevented him from urinating. We moved Flame to a paddock where Dr. P. attempted to sedate him so he could treat the infected area. Despite staggering and going down, Flame struggled to his feet over and over again even while I sat on his shoulder or neck. It became clear that if he were set on standing up, he would stand up.

Flame fought sedation with an iron will, and his reeling brought him outside the paddock onto the gravel driveway where he continued to fall and stand up. I watched in tears as my horse ripped open his knees and bled after falling to the ground again and again. As darkness replaced twilight, and the floodlights failed to provide enough illumination to be of any use, Dr. P. gave up and told me he would return the next day and try again. We moved Flame into his stall where he continued to stand on unsteady legs.

I talked to Mrs. A. after Dr. P. left and told her what had happened. She instructed me to be at the barn early the next morning, and Jessie would drive Flame and me out to New Bolton, the unparalleled veterinary clinic at the University of Pennsylvania. Mrs. A. would contact Dr. P. for me, and she would call my manager at Bell Labs to explain the situation to her. The degree of compassion evidenced by Mrs. A. while I crumpled with anxiety was priceless.

The long ride out to Pennsylvania could have been terrible for me, giving me time to think the worst possible scenarios about Flame. But Jessie regaled me with all kinds of horse stories, the details of her accident, and anecdotes about her growing up. I've always wished I had been blessed with that same easy gift of gab.

We arrived at New Bolton, unloaded Flame, and proceeded inside a hospital unlike anything I'd ever seen. No wonder the facility is renowned the world over! Besides being enormous with what seemed like its own horizon, the vast amount of equipment blew my mind. And to see so many large animals—horses, sheep, cows—being treated at once, some contained in individual pens, some being led about, some hanging in huge slings to keep pressure off injured body parts...I had the sense of intruding upon a magical world, the elite world of veterinary medicine in which I, a mere mortal, had no business. How to gain passage into such a world?

While I groped for a grasp on reality, a veterinary student took Flame from me and assured me that my horse would be fine. I could even watch as they treated Flame. He led the horse to a restraining pen where a team sedated him in minutes, and in less than an hour, removed the summer sore and treated his knees which had sustained only superficial injuries. The student returned Flame to me with the prognosis that Flame would have no more trouble peeing. He instructed me to hose down his knees twice a day, apply some kind of prescribed salve to them, and rewrap them in clean gauze after each cleaning. Follow this procedure for at least a week. Feelings of relief that Flame was returned to health and that his injured knees required no elaborate treatment heightened my wistful thoughts of wanting to hang around the facility longer so I could continue to observe all the extraordinary work being performed. Oh, and as a result of my wise decision to have Flame insured when I bought him, I paid a grand total of fifty dollars for the entire New Bolton experience.

Over the next week, every morning before work and every afternoon after work, I removed Flame's knee dressing, led him out to the hose by the driveway, and flushed out his wounds. I then applied the medicine and rewrapped his knees. I watched Flame's wounds heal and the hair grow back over the injuries, and I felt like a veterinarian. Mrs. A. caught up with me sometime later and offered one of the highest compliments I'd ever received. She said, "You may not be the best rider yet or know as much about horses as some people do, but after watching the dedication with which you cared for Flame, I would trust my horses with you anytime."

BAREBACK

Arabian horses have a given smooth gait and a broad back without spiny ridges—perfect for riding bareback if you know how, which I didn't, and lacked the nerve to try until our first winter together when a foot of wind-driven snow had fallen leaving three-foot high drifts. I went to see Flame after the snow had stopped and the roads had been plowed, put his bridle on him, and led him into the ring. After clearing snow from one of the mounting blocks, I sat upon him for the first time without a saddle. I figured if I fell off, I'd land in a snowdrift and be unhurt. Because I rode with an English saddle, as opposed to a Western saddle with a higher back, a deeper seat, and a pommel in front, I felt strange sitting on him bareback only because I had no stirrups in which to anchor my feet. When I asked him to walk with a squeeze of my knees, I felt as if I were in a rocking chair. The depth of snow prevented Flame from moving into a trot, but that didn't stop me from reveling in the sweet thought that I had reached new heights in horsemanship.

ONCE TOO OFTEN

Fall, despite being a period of nature's decay, has been my favorite season of the year for as long as I can remember. The changing colors of the leaves, the drier, cooler temperatures, the harbinger of the holiday season… The seasonal changes affected my horse, too. Aggressive deer flies no longer tormented him by stinging his flanks or buzzing around his ears. And he moved into an extended trot or a faster canter with just the slightest signal from me, almost as if he sensed what I would ask before I asked. In short, Flame was full of boundless spirit and fun, and I enjoyed some of my best rides as we set off with him tossing his head and high-stepping, sometimes sideways, through the woods.

The only sure thing that could, and often did, ruin otherwise perfect rides was the sound of gunshots when hunting season began. They saddened me, and they scared Flame, who would spook whenever he heard the crack of gunfire. One brisk late-November morning during our second year together, I just had to get in a quick ride around the paddock before I headed into work. It was sublime, and brought to mind John Sebastian's "What a Day for a Daydream." *BANG!* Reverie shattered.

Flame spooked to the right as always, and I fell to the left as always. As the saddle shifted from under me and I became airborne, my right foot did not release from the stirrup as it should have. I felt my right knee twist and jerk my foot free as I fell to the ground. Not a lot of pain that I remember, but I looked at my leg bent as I'd never seen it bent. And I knew without a doubt that it would not support me if I attempted to put weight on it. I tried anyway and, as expected, crumpled to the ground. Flame, by this time, had come back to me and was looking at me as if to say, "Well, come on. Get up and get back on me. You've done this enough times in the past."

Instead, I pulled myself up by the saddle girth, draped an arm around Flame's neck for support and hopped back to the barn. I somehow returned Flame to his stall and then called Steve from the barn telephone, probably waking him up. "I'm hurt." Steve later told me that when he heard those words, he thought, "Houston, we have a problem."

He called the ambulance for me and arrived at the barn while the EMTs worked on me. I think there must be something unwritten and untaught in the EMT training modules that compels first aiders to evaluate an injury by cutting away clothing with scissors before checking for zippers or buttons that might allow for garment removal the easy and old-fashioned way. I wore a pair of leather chaps that morning, and here came the scissors.

"*No!*"

I indicated the zippers that ran the length of each leg but to avoid hurt feelings, I compromised and allowed them to cut away the leg of my jeans before transporting me to Morristown Hospital.

A battery of x-rays confirmed that I'd torn almost every ligament and tendon in the knee, and the orthopedic surgeon on duty, Dr. Crutchlow (yes, that really was his name), informed me that under-the-knife surgery would be required. Not the arthroscopic kind. Conflicting emotions stirred within me at the prospect of undergoing general anesthesia. I could really get into the loopy rush I felt just before I passed out as I'd learned from an appendectomy and cosmetic oral surgery. Recovery from surgery, however, was always ugly. I got sick as soon as I woke up proving that no good time, not even anesthesia, comes without cost.

As anticipated, Christmas that year was difficult for me. Instead of hours spent decorating my tree with anal intensity, I spent endless hours on the sofa painting wooden ornaments and stringing popcorn and cranberries. Steve did most of the actual decorating under my watchful eye and, as I remember, the tree ended up looking great in a rustic kind of way. Christmas shopping was kept to a minimum (no Internet yet), but we ventured out to the mall one night where Steve navigated a crutch-wielding me without incident through holiday shoppers. We went to church Christmas Eve. And because everyone goes to church on that holy night, including those who are handicapped, the nearest parking space to the church we could find had me bumping along on my crutches for at least a block. All those hours mucking Flame's stall paid off in terms of upper arm strength.

About a month after surgery, the doc removed my plaster cast, and I got to see the surgical wound on the inside of my knee for the first time. It was a scary, red, ugly six- or seven-inch thing that looked like a giant bug with all those black stitches. After he'd removed the stitches, it just looked red and ugly. Doc covered the wound with a fiberglass cast, which was lighter than the plaster one had been but not as comfortable. It didn't wrap around under my foot, so it kind of bounced up and down on my ankle bone as I walked.

Getting into and out of the bathtub for a shower with a full cast encased in a large trash bag and sealed with duct tape was a trick worthy of Houdini. When I lost the fiberglass cast as well, the doc fitted me with a snazzy hinged knee brace in preparation for weeks of physical therapy. PT was a bear as is most PT, but the immediate gratification achieved by the removal of my cast was the ability to soak in a bath unbagged! Blessed rapture! No more facsimiles of showers attempted in abject fear that, despite wrapping my leg securely in plastic, water would somehow find its way between the cast and my skin. As I reveled in a euphoric soak, my first in more than two months, I saw that my injured leg resembled that of an emaciated plucked chicken, atrophied, white and flaky... and hairy. Gross. And as I'd been warned, the knee and surrounding areas were numb and would remain so for a short but indeterminate length of time. Broad new vistas of trust in my eyesight and the steadiness of my hand opened when I first attempted to shave my knee. Let me tell you, until you've shaved a part of your body that you cannot feel, you've missed out on a real thrill.

Staples and bailing wire now stabilize my right knee, which has required several arthroscopic surgeries to repair one meniscus or another since the initial injury. Maniacal games of racquetball and my propensity for tripping over objects (real or imagined) take their toll on a compromised knee. These subsequent surgeries have been in-and-out deals requiring local anesthesia and maybe two days of recuperation. Good to go. I had my last such surgery in 2001, seventeen years ago.

I didn't see Flame during my crutch-wielding time, but Steve and Mrs. A. assured me that he was being well cared for and ridden by Terry once or twice a week. When I did return to the barn while wearing the brace, Flame looked as healthy as ever and welcomed me with a nicker, looked for an apple, and let me hug him and groom him.

I returned to work in March and resumed my normal routine with Flame. We took many rides together, and I again experienced the simple joy of being alone with nature while the real world ceased to exist. But I never again felt as relaxed upon him as I once had.

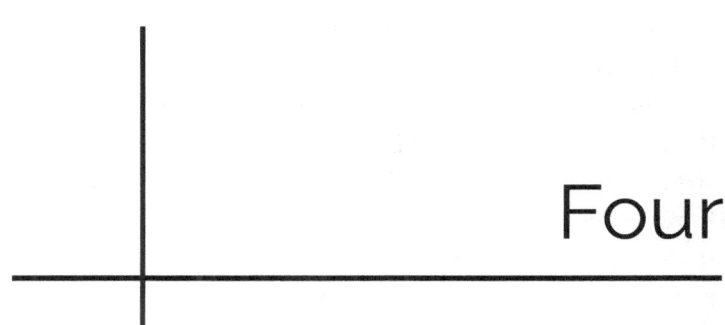

Four

I need to backtrack a bit here to my first Christmas with Steve. An official horse owner on paper, if not in person yet, I presented Steve with horseback riding lessons having no idea if he even liked or would like horseback riding. What I did know was that I would need some lessons before Flame and I could enjoy each other, and I wanted Steve to take lessons with me, to share to some extent in my joy of owning a horse. Being the good sport and gracious person he was, he accepted the lessons with a smile and some weeks later, enrolled in classes with me at Snowbird Acres Farm.

We spent our first Christmas holiday in Ohio with his parents whom I hadn't met yet. Talk about scary delights! Steve times three! Three times the intelligence and three times the dry, rough-around-the-edges humor, and all on their home turf! I consider myself a fairly intelligent woman but simply put, the Frysinger clan made mincemeat of me, and in a hurry, too. I remember my first conversation with his Mom. We somehow got to talking about sake, and my blank stare tipped her off to the fact that I had never heard of sake. She turned to Steve who was sitting in the living room with us, cocked her head toward me, and asked, "Where did you find this one?" Steve, without a moment's hesitation, answered, "I picked her up on the street," to which his Mom replied, "Must've been a very quiet street." Game on. Ma Frysinger 1, Stormie 0. The guffaws at my (and Steve's) expense continued Christmas morning as I opened my stocking from Steve and showed off a hoof pick, lunge line and riding crop.

Steve and I began our riding lessons in January. Five or six students of beginner/intermediate levels filled out our class. Julie, our instructor, was a delightful older woman maybe in her late fifties or early sixties, but sharp as a tack with the perfect personality for instilling trust and confidence in her students. After a couple of lessons, Julie believed me to be capable of handling a younger, more spirited horse and assigned Nobel´ to me. Made me feel more than a little smug. But pride does indeed go before a fall!

We were learning to jump, and Julie had set up some cross rails and low horizontals. I watched the students before me clear the jumps. It came my turn and as I cantered up to the jump while entertaining the lofty delusion of winning everything in sight at hunter-class shows, Nobel´ balked at the first cross rail. I sailed over his head and landed on the ground in a heap, embarrassed but unhurt. Julie encouraged me to get right back on and try again. This time, smooth as silk. Smugness was nowhere to be found.

My riding skill and comfort level on horseback continued to improve, as did those of Steve who also enjoyed the lessons. I could sit to the trot, switch diagonals, ask the horse to change leads at the canter, and jump low hurdles with no problem. But I could not get the hang of posting. Julie said I worked too hard and advised me over and over to let the horse do the work by "throwing" me out of the saddle so that all I had to do was a little hip-thrust while in the air. In desperation, I think, Julie offered me private lessons on her old Clydesdale, Tom Thumb. Imagine learning to post on a Clydesdale! Tom was enormous! But he was a steady and gentle beast and after a few sessions together, he helped me figure out the mechanics of posting.

As an aside, I have a keen sense of ESP, but one that I can neither channel nor control. It presents itself as gnawing, powerful and unexplained anxious feelings, sometimes accompanied by images. Occurrences validating said feelings have happened often enough that they no longer surprise me, and people who know me well accept them and respect them as part and parcel of my spirit. Minor case in point: when I felt a nagging urge to read all the sympathy cards in a greeting card store the day before the Oklahoma City bombing.

One snowy winter morning as Steve and I readied for our riding lesson, I experienced a persistent feeling of foreboding—one that I could tell stemmed from something other than nervousness about road conditions. We arrived at Snowbird without incident and saw that we and one other woman whom I'd never seen were the only ones at class. Because of the snow, our lesson took place that day inside the Kentucky barn—a barn designed like a "reverse doughnut" in that the stalls were clustered in the middle, and a rectangular indoor track ran around the outside of the stalls. A couple of Snowbird staff were cleaning stalls and feeding the horses not being used in our lesson. Lots of talk and laughter among the girls tending the animals, but our mounts took it all in stride.

Julie had us riding around the track counter-clockwise, one at a time, at the trot and canter with our hands off the reins and our arms held out shoulder height to the side. We'd gone through the rotation a few times with me always the last to ride. The lesson drew near its close, and the other two school horses were returned to their respective stalls. So here I go riding my last lap, more or less posting to the trot with my arms out to the side, watching my posture, keeping my heels down, and again imagining myself as some world-class champion rider. This happy fantasy continued until I rounded one corner and saw an unhaltered horse standing in the middle of the track. I reined in my horse, a big Palomino named Trigger (what else?), and watched in fear and amazement as the girls ran around the horse helter skelter rather than acting in a sensible manner by filling a bucket with oats and encouraging the horse to return to its stall. Julie and the other two students could not see what was happening on my side of the "dough-nut," nor could they see that I had stopped.

The uncontrolled horse, having had enough of the craziness, took off at an easy trot in a counter-clockwise direction away from me and disappeared around the corner. With the other horse out of sight, I dismounted Trigger and put him in the nearest empty stall, all thoughts of world-class champion obliterated by a white-hot intangible premonition and terrible half-formed blood-soaked images flashing through my mind, much like slasher movie stills.

By this time, the other horse had rounded another corner and approached the closed barn door where Julie, Steve, and the other student stood. The sight of an untethered horse coming toward them alerted everyone that something was wrong, and they all walked over to the aisle where the girls continued to run around in confusion and where I stood against the outside wall watching my movie stills. The untethered horse reversed direction at some point because it reappeared, this time coming toward us from the corner around which it had disappeared a few seconds earlier.

Julie walked into the center of the track and spread her arms wide in front of the horse. But rather than stopping as anticipated, the horse continued its slow trot and bumped Julie, knocking her down and into the interior wall of stalls before stopping and standing still. Steve and I watched the scene unfold from a safe distance, but when Julie appeared dazed from the collision, Steve approached her to help her to her feet. The other student also moved over to Julie. I, who knew nothing of first aid, cowered in a corner and hoped nothing worse would happen. While Steve and the woman bent over Julie, the horse shifted a little, and the woman started to stand and smacked the horse on the rump to move the horse away. In response to the slap, the horse kicked, and its rear hoof caught the woman in the forehead, opening a gash that bled profusely as all head injuries do.

Things happened in a hurry. Steve, who knew first aid, turned his attention to the injured woman and applied light pressure with his bandana to her wound. The woman's husband who had been sitting unnoticed on a tack box during the lesson, walked around to us, became distraught at the sight of his wife lying on the floor bleeding, and demanded that the horse be shot. Julie, standing and unhurt, called for an ambulance from the barn telephone. And the stable girls figured out to lure the horse into its stall with a bucket of oats.

Betting that the injured woman would file a lawsuit against Snowbird, Steve and I wrote up separate detailed accounts of what we'd witnessed as soon as we returned home. Sure enough, some weeks later, we both received a Deposition Subpoena for Personal Appearance on behalf of the plaintiff. So, on the date and time specified in the subpoena, Steve and I each took the day off from work, drove to court with our respective statements, and waited…for a long time…before an attorney approached us, thanked us for coming, and informed us that the case had been settled in arbitration. Our depositions would not be required, and we could leave to make the most of what remained of the day.

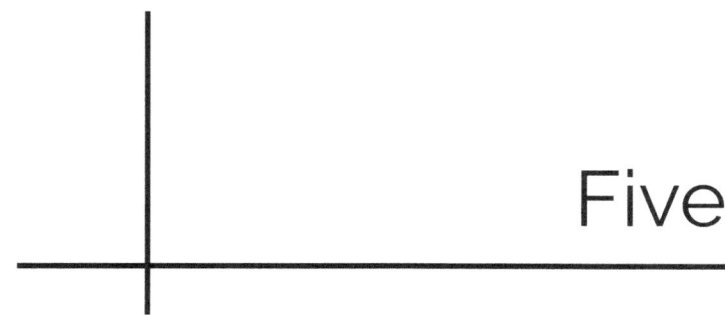

Five

Ownership of Flame failed to extinguish my desire to be a vet tech, and one day when the fire burned hotter than usual, I arranged to spend a day with a local veterinarian and his technician to observe eight hours in a working practice. I was psyched, and the experience did not disappoint. I greeted clients and their pets, wiped down examination tables, assisted with simple surgeries, and watched in fascination at the more complicated operations.

One procedure proved difficult for me to observe: the declawing of a cat. Even then, I found the operation barbaric, the equivalent of cutting off a human finger at the first knuckle. That many states have banned declawing makes me happy, and I hope all states will follow suit. It can't happen too soon.

I watched the vet's technician neuter several male cats in under an hour. The relative simplicity of the operation amazed me. After watching a couple of such procedures, I thought to myself, "I could do that!" Only later did it occur to me that the clients paid for the services of a veterinarian, and a technician had no legal or ethical right to perform such surgery.

I watched the vet spay a German Shepherd, a much more complicated surgery than castration. And I watched him amputate one front leg of a kitten that had been hit by a car. Not only did I enjoy a chock-full-of-wonderful-experiences day in a veterinarian's office, but I learned something new about myself as well: My normal squeamishness at the sight of blood or injury to an animal takes a back seat to my focus on treating the animal and how I might assist a veterinarian.

At the end of the day, more convinced than ever that I wanted to spend my life in the service of a veterinarian, I bounced into our kitchen and chortled at Steve, "I think I could perform a castration." I don't remember Steve's exact words in response to this gleeful declaration, but I doubt they were, "Really? Show me!"

Six

When driving home from dinner one evening, Steve and I saw what looked like an injured rabbit in the street. Steve began to slow the car even before I asked him to stop. And before he could object, I had jumped from the car and run to look at the rabbit that kind of hopped in slow circles. I scooped it up without trouble, an indication that it was indeed hurt although I saw no obvious signs of injury.

Steve supported me as we drove home with the rabbit in my lap and called Dr. P, a friend and an old-fashioned country-style vet— the same vet who had attempted to sedate Flame the previous year. I explained the situation to Dr. P. and asked if we could bring the rabbit over to him right away despite the late hour (I'm thinking 9:00). Yes, of course, we could.

When we arrived at the office, which was set up in the basement of his house, I placed the rabbit on the table so Dr. P. could examine it. Dr. P. knew I entertained ideas of becoming a vet tech and took time to explain in detail the rabbit's condition. He indicated how one eye bulged and looked upward, while the other eye appeared normal—a sure sign of brain damage. Dr. P. also assured me that the rabbit was too far gone to be feeling any pain.

He manipulated the rabbit's legs with care and showed me how one of the femurs and pelvic bones had been broken, which explained why the rabbit moved in circles when I approached it in the street. He offered to let me move the leg as well. Total fascination with the rabbit's injuries, my interaction with the vet, and a feeling of "so this is what it's all about" replaced the sadness I'd felt when we first arrived at Dr. P.'s office. I knew then and there that I would apply to Michigan State University for entry into their Veterinary Technician program.

After Dr. P. had put the animal into forever sleep with no charge to me, I looked behind me at Steve who had remained silent during the examination of the rabbit. And I had to smile when I saw this 6'3" man, an Eagle Scout, a motorcyclist, and a former first-aider leaning against the counter for support, having turned a pale shade of green and looking like he would pass out. He told me later that he admired the way I, who became nauseated by any kind of animal discomfort, got right in there and worked with the rabbit while he had felt his own knees turn to gelatin.

Soon after the rabbit incident, I applied to MSU, scored well on their ACT tests, and was accepted into their Vet Tech Program—with a caveat. Isn't there always! Before I could consider myself an official Spartan, I needed to pass a college-level chemistry course since I'd never taken even one chemistry course in high school. So then began a frustrating series of attempts and failures on my part as I spent many dollars and much time in several colleges and universities trying to meet MSU's condition for my entry into the program. But, despite an arsenal of willing chemistry tutors at Bell Labs, I could not balance an equation, could not pass a chemistry course, and never became a vet tech. I did, however, pass an online Veterinary Assistant course decades later after I'd retired from the corporate world, and I remain hopeful that God will find a way yet to employ me in a vet's office.

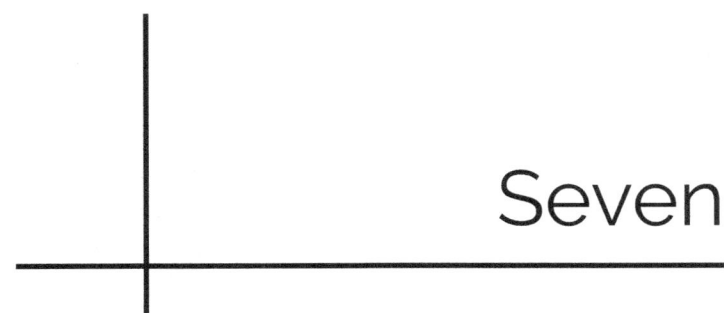

Seven

Life crashed around me. By mid-1984, Steve and I found ourselves unhappy more often than happy together even though neither of us admitted it for a long time. A telling indicator of our changing relationship occurred when we discussed a choice between us taking a trip to France or installing a new kitchen. I opted for the kitchen, which turned out for the best. When Steve sold the house the following year after I'd moved out, the new kitchen allowed him to make a hefty profit. And for that, I was happy.

Before the house was sold, when I could delude myself no longer about the way things were, when blinding reality forced me to accept that Steve and I really were on the verge of calling it quits, I knew I would have to sell Flame. Steve never once hinted that I would have to sell him, but I knew I wouldn't be able to keep a horse once I began paying rent on my own place. And I knew that selling him would be one of the hardest things I'd ever have to do.

It was imperative that I find him a good home, so I didn't want to wait until the eleventh hour to sell him. One young woman who came to look at Flame early on was willing to meet my asking price of five thousand dollars. From the moment she approached me in her fancy riding boots and breeches, and carrying a riding crop, I doubted I would sell him to her. But I allowed her to ride him and watched her pull the reins short as she moved Flame into the ring. And I watched Flame fret, toss his head, and kick out his heels as his rider demanded moves from him that he didn't understand, using the crop when he failed to perform to her liking. When she dismounted, she said something to the effect of, "I could work with him, but he's certainly not safe for an inexperienced rider." One or two other people came to look at Flame, but there was no connection. Flame was too small. He wasn't experienced enough to show. He was a gelding, not a stallion. My price was too high. I began to feel desperate.

The relationship between Steve and me, while never hostile, continued to deteriorate. And I still hadn't found a suitable buyer for Flame. I asked Mrs. A. and Jessie and others at the barn if they knew anyone who might be interested in a seven-year old Arab gelding. I notified veterinarians in the area of my situation and dropped my price down to three figures. My phone still didn't ring. Until one day a woman called saying she and her husband had been considering buying a horse for their young boys and had heard about Flame from their vet. We set up a time for Joanne and her husband to stop by and look at Flame. The couple showed up in jeans and sneakers, and neither carried a crop. The husband wanted to ride Flame around the ring, and I watched with sad relief as Flame dropped his head and moved through his paces without issue. I had found my buyers.

They understood my heartbreak at selling Flame and invited me to come see their property in Harding Township, a genteel town where many families owned horses. I accepted their offer and saw a well-kept small shaded paddock and a two-horse barn. The children were young (maybe seven or eight years old), so I figured they wouldn't outgrow Flame, at least not while he himself was young. My single concern was that there were no other horses to keep Flame company, but Joanne told me they planned to buy another horse in the near future. I got good vibes from the whole setup and told them I would sell Flame to them. I would include his bridle which had an easy bit, and some of his blankets if I could visit him and ride him once in a while. And if they would sign an agreement to sell him back to me at the same price they paid for him if, for any reason, they decided not to keep him. Joanne signed without hesitation.

I bade Flame a tearful farewell the night before he was to be moved, but I could not be at the barn to see him taken away.

I did, however, go to visit and ride him twice over the next few months. He looked happy and healthy. On my third visit, it was clear that Flame didn't remember me. I never returned, and I never saw Flame again.

A couple of years later, I saw Joanne at a gas station where we were both having our cars serviced. She recognized me first, reintroduced herself, and told me Flame was doing well. He was in 4H with her boys. And they'd bought another horse a while back. I was welcome to come visit, but I knew in my heart that I would never take her up on her invitation.

When I sold Flame, I kept my saddle and my old tack trunk in which I stored one of his blankets and various ointments and accessories. I haul the trunk out of our storage room from time to time just to open it and bury my nose in the blanket…and remember.

Eight

Both my parents suffered from a near-total lack of integrity, as well as a complete lack of compassion and sound judgment. One of my clearest memories that validates such sterling description happened when I was maybe ten years old. I had brought home a kitten from a litter that one of the neighborhood kids' cat had had and asked if we could keep it. My mother didn't like cats, but my father thought the animal resembled a cat he had while growing up. We kept it.

Chessie, as my father named the kitten, was a sweet, soft, long-haired white and multiple-shades-of-gray creature. She was beautiful. I don't remember how long we had Chessie, but it wasn't very long. And I don't remember any play time with her at all, probably because such time didn't exist. My father, paranoid by nature, would have quashed any activity that hinted at the possibility of Chessie bonding more with my younger sister or me than with him, even though both he and my mother paid little attention to the kitten after she'd been with us a couple of days. What I do remember is hearing my mother complain that the kitten had grown fat and lazy. It never occurred to her that maybe they should feed her less and pay some attention to her.

Then one morning, my parents piled my younger sister Kathy and me into the cigarette-smoke-filled car along with a box containing Chessie. I didn't know where we were going or what was about to happen, but we wound up on some desolate road alongside a big field. I watched from the back seat as my father took the box with Chessie in it, carried it into the field, removed the kitten from the box, set her down, and walked away from her. He then turned the car around and drove away. I looked out the rear window and thought how small and alone Chessie looked. And I can't unsee that image.

I didn't understand at the time what had happened. No one had prepared me for the fact that Chessie would no longer be a part of our household or that we would abandon her in a field. And no one comforted me. The saddest thing is that I don't remember crying. I think I was so accustomed to living with a sense of emptiness and neglect that I was used to it. Tears served no purpose. But to this day, I resent that my parents subjected Kathy and me to that experience rather than at least dropping us off with my grandmother to spare us the trauma of seeing our pet discarded like an unwanted piece of furniture. And today, I can cry over losing Chessie.

History repeated itself, in a sense, decades later. My father had died some years before, and my mother had moved to Ohio where she lived by herself but near my sister. She called me one day while I was at work and told me she had brought a kitten home from a local shelter a few weeks ago.

"Why?" I asked her with equal parts surprise and anger. "You don't even like cats."

"I was lonely and wanted company." Hmm, okay. I felt depressed after the conversation, and a nagging worry about the kitten my mother had adopted gnawed at my gut.

A few weeks later, I received another phone call from my mother—two phone calls within as many months—an unprecedented record. For the last several years, one conversation in a twelve-month period with her would have been considered a lot and more than enough. I asked her about the kitten.

"I got rid of it. Took it back to the shelter."

My heart broke, and I struggled for calm against rising fury. When I asked why she had done something so unthinking and cruel, she responded without a hint of remorse. "It drove me crazy. It was swinging on my curtains and clawing at the furniture." Really? Thoughts of condemnation drove their way to the forefront of my consciousness. What did you expect? That's what kittens do. Why didn't you buy her a scratching post? Some toys? Why didn't you spend time with her and play with her? You said you got her because you wanted company.

"You ruined any chance for that animal to have a permanent home. And you probably condemned it to death," I choked.

I hung up and felt the familiar cold clingy depression lurking just behind my consciousness, threatening to suck me in as it always did after dealing with that woman. I fought it off, but I never forgave my mother for the selfishness of her actions in destroying the life of that animal. And I think I realized then, perhaps for the first time, how much I hated her.

I spoke to my mother maybe once or twice again before she died. I don't know. Perhaps I've tried to forget. I didn't attend her funeral (or that of my father) and, despite dire warnings from well-meaning friends, I have never regretted passing on the opportunity to bid either of them a final fond farewell.

But for the last several years, I've struggled with trying to accept that my mother was a mentally ill woman powerless to help herself. She was one of those unfortunate people (as was my father) who was incapable of marshalling the necessary time, patience, and compassion required after accepting responsibility for another living creature, be it child or animal. Perhaps the needs of a goldfish would have better suited my parents' ability to sacrifice of themselves: feed them once a day, clean their water every week, forget about them.

My constant petition to God is that He will enable me to forgive my parents for the harm they inflicted upon me. I can't find the strength or the will to do so on my own. And God hears me, because He has provided me the desire to *want* to forgive.

Nine

When one person blesses another with some random act of kindness, the memory of such act sometimes roots itself forever in the recipient's memory. I will never forget the time a stranger came to my door and offered to perform what seemed like a miracle to a brokenhearted me.

I rented a cottage in Chester, New Jersey sometime around 2000 on a quiet semi-paved road with 15 acres of woods and fields for my backyard. My nearest neighbor lived half a football field away on the same property, but in the main house. The cottage had once been the servants' quarters, and it was perfect for me. Surrounded by full-grown maples and oaks, it was easy to imagine myself in a rain forest during heavy downpours when the branches and dripping leaves hung low and blocked my view of the road.

Chester is a small town, and it isn't uncommon for shopkeepers and patrons to be on a first-name basis with each other. Danny, the owner of a local pet store who knew me from when I bought food for my ferrets, one day asked me if I might be interested in a sweet, housebroken, three-year-old black Lab. Ricky was "free to a good home," the owners being unable to keep him—his boisterous Lab-type personality caused concern for the safety of their newborn baby. I had considered visiting the local animal shelters in search of a dog. But the idea of having one fall into my lap, as well as having a chance to meet the previous owners, seemed too perfect to pass up. I collected Ricky the following Friday evening from his house so I'd have all weekend with him before returning to work on Monday. Another positive, he traveled well in the car without a crate.

As soon as we arrived home, I walked him around the cottage and into the woods. I took him out again later that night. Then, given the relative remoteness of the cottage and the minimal traffic on our road, especially at 10:00 p.m., I took a chance and unleashed him. He ran off. After twenty minutes of calling his name and looking for him in the dark with only a flashlight for illumination, I returned inside realizing I'd made a stupid mistake and admitting, too, that I'd made it out of sheer laziness. I didn't want to have to walk a dog every couple of hours when I had acres of property around me on which he could roam. And then I heard a dog bark! I ran to the back door, and there stood Ricky, tail wagging, grinning from ear to ear as if to say after seeing the relief on my face, "What's wrong, Mama? I just wanted to check out all the new smells and maybe scare up a deer to chase." From then on, I had no worries about Ricky disappearing. He was home, and he knew it.

Ricky was a good soul, but our first night together caused me to doubt the wisdom of my impulsive decision to adopt him. I did not own a crate, and I trusted him not to mess the house or chew what didn't belong to him. What I hadn't anticipated were his over-the-top anxiety and restlessness in new surroundings.

The cottage had an unconventional floorplan with the bedroom off the kitchen, and the foyer, living room and bathroom off to the other side of the bedroom. The bedroom was carpeted; the kitchen and foyer were not. When I turned out the lights to go to sleep that first night, Ricky, instead of curling up on the old comforter I'd laid on the floor near my bed, paced back and forth for hours. I would hear the "click, click, click" of his toenails on the kitchen floor, then silence as he walked through the bedroom, then the "click, click, click" of his toenails in the foyer, then silence and "click, click, click" again as he returned to the kitchen. Over and over again. The sound of finger-nails scraping on a blackboard could not have set my nerves more on edge than listening to the sound of Ricky doing laps through my cot-tage. By God's grace, he calmed down after that first night, and I was spared the necessity and expense of having to buy a crate for him. Not to mention the possibility of becoming psychotic from lack of sleep.

It wasn't long before I could leave Ricky outside and untethered all day while I was at work. He always had a bowl of water available to him, and he had shelter underneath the tool shed located a stone's throw from the house. And always when I returned home at 5:30 in the evening, Ricky would be waiting for me outside the front door and come running to greet me with big hugs and sloppy kisses.

One Saturday morning after feeding Ricky his breakfast, I re-leased him for his routine toilet and recognizance of the previous night's clandestine comings and goings of wild things in and around our woods. When Ricky did not return by early afternoon, I figured he'd found some comfortable patch of pine needles and had settled down to sleep in the summer heat. Or maybe he'd picked up the scent of a fox new to the neighborhood. But when the skies darkened and I heard thunder in the distance, I whistled and called for Ricky. Still nothing. *Sheesh!* Ricky had been known to ignore my voice in the past, and I knew a free spirit was part of his Lab DNA. And he was used to being outside all day, every day, while I worked, rain or shine. Couldn't blame him for his unwillingness to jump at my beck and call just because I happened to be around for a change. But the rain had begun to fall in sheets, and I began to worry in earnest when he didn't return for his mid-afternoon treat which he always received when I was home. A built-in alarm clock telling him it was time to eat was also part of Ricky's DNA.

The all-too-often-justified sense of foreboding that I knew well and that had been mounting since mid-morning, now threatened to intensify into a full-scale panic attack. Yielding to the intangible but absolute conviction that something was wrong, I headed out into the rain to search for Ricky. I found him lying around the bend by the side of the road at the edge of the woods, lifeless, but still warm with no apparent internal or external injuries. I stood over him, paralyzed by shock and a complete lack of direction as to what to do.

My senses recorded nothing more than the sound of the torrential rain through the leaves and the sight of the still dog on the pavement. At some point, I realized I was soaked to the skin having not grabbed my poncho before I left the house. I returned to the cottage, my head filled with nagging questions which would never be answered. Why was my dog dead? Had he eaten something he shouldn't have? Been bitten by some small venomous creature? And the big question: What should I do with him? I wanted to bury him, but how and where? Almost a given, my landlord would not approve the burial of a dog on his property. I paced the floors much as Ricky had done that first night.

Another crash of thunder. No, a knock on the front door. I opened the door and saw a young man whom I'd never before met. He wore a blue shirt, had light-colored hair and beard, kind eyes, and he was dripping wet. Interesting how certain details stick in one's mind.

He said to me, "I saw your dog on the road outside." How did he know that I had belonged to Ricky? I never thought to ask. The stranger at my door continued, "I have a farm in Long Valley. Would you like me to take him with me in my truck and bury him for you on my property?" I looked up toward the street and saw what I assumed to be his pickup truck parked next to my car. Relief and gratitude flooded through me. How does one thank a man—a stranger—for a gift of such magnitude? So simple in its expression but so profound in its generosity and ramifications…and so perfect in its form. I never even asked this Good Samaritan his name. And I never saw him again.

But so long as I live, I'll believe that the stranger in the blue shirt with the kind eyes was an answer to a prayer I hadn't even known I'd prayed.

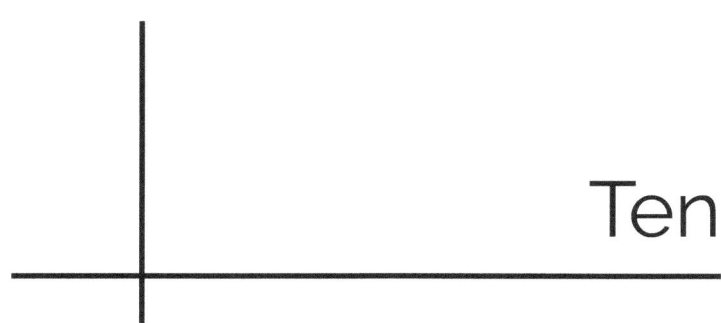

Ten

I recognized the sound of a rattlesnake's warning for what it was the first time I heard it: an imperative demand to move. The rattle is loud, cold, and absolute. It leaves no room for hesitation or discussion.

My Chester cottage included in its backyard a very large and dense wineberry patch, those wild raspberry-type fruits that pop during late July or early August. I looked forward to harvesting them every year and enjoying them over vanilla ice cream or eating them by the handful right off the bushes—hadn't yet learned how to make wineberry jam. The bushes yielded quarts of berries, even with the birds, deer, and other wild creatures sharing in the bounty. Decked out in light-colored pants, a long-sleeved white shirt, white socks, a broad-brimmed hat, and gardening gloves, and having spritzed myself with insect repellant, I'd make my way out to the berry bushes...and indulge my country girl spirit. I would skirt the edges of the bushes and then blaze my way into the thorny thicket to get the hard-to-reach berries. As a result of my greedy endeavors and despite all my anti-tick precautions, I acquired deer tick hitchhikers on a regular basis. I would find so many of them on me that my doctor took to prescribing antibiotics for me, beginning sometime in May and continuing through late August as a preventative measure against my contracting Lyme disease. I don't condone taking preventative antibiotics as a rule, but in my case, it was the expedient procedure to follow.

One day early on in my berry collecting, I waded into the bushes and heard *The Rattle!* The bushes were too many and too dense for me to see where the snake lay, but I knew without a doubt that one shared the patch with me, and it sounded close. Really close. Like right beside me! I froze. And for some reason as I stood there, I remembered my father telling me how he had been bitten in the leg by a rattlesnake and had to cut an X into the wound to release the venom. The image of cutting an X into myself played and replayed itself in my head and complicated any attempt by me to evaluate my immediate situation. As fate would have it, I had not ventured too far into the bushes, but still just a little too deep for me to take one giant step backward to safety. The *Rattle* continued, and I realized I couldn't even tell from what direction it came other than from somewhere at my feet. I weighed what appeared to be my only choices: back out and chance tripping over branches trailing on the ground and increase the risk of further aggravating the snake, or turn around and walk out frontward and increase the risk of further aggravating the snake, or continue deeper into the bushes and increase the risk of further aggravating the snake. I opted for column A. The *Rattle* sounded deafening in its urgency. Since it was apparent that I made the snake no happier by remaining where I stood, I took one deliberate, as-long-as-I-dared step back. Not bitten yet. A second step landed one foot outside the bushes onto the lawn. I brought my other foot out. The *Rattle* ceased, but my heart beat a rumba in my chest. From the safety of the lawn, I crouched down and peered into the bushes to see if I could spot the snake, but either it had slithered away in silence after the perceived danger of my presence passed, or it remained where it was so well camouflaged in the branches and dead leaves that I never caught sight of it. A close encounter of the most exquisite kind, and one which I hope to never repeat.

I did see a rattlesnake in the flesh once while driving home from hiking the wooded trails of Stokes Forest with my friend Hester. The snake lay sunning itself in the middle of the highway, and because I was afraid it would get hit by a car, I pulled over to the shoulder and walked back to it. Hester followed me with admonitions to be careful. I had zero idea what I would do when I reached the snake, but I hoped people would be more apt to swerve away from it if they saw a human standing beside it. Such a gorgeous copper-and-green-colored creature maybe three inches in diameter and four feet long! I was again amazed by the loudness of the snake's rattle warning me to stay back. No problem, but I continued to stand in the middle of Route 206 wondering how to move it out of harm's way without getting myself bitten or hit by a car traveling at 50 MPH.

No cell phones yet.

I lost track of time while I remained mesmerized by the appearance and sound of the snake. It occurred to me later how odd it was that of all the cars that passed us, not one stopped either to gawk or to offer assistance—until a park ranger drove up, pulled over, and approached us with a long stick. He asked if I'd like to see the snake strike. Strike who? "Yes," I answered out loud. The ranger poked the snake with the stick, and I thought to myself, "The snake won't strike a stick; there's no heat in it." I told the ranger I just wanted the snake out of the road before it came to any harm. He continued prodding the snake until it moved off to the shoulder where it stopped and coiled itself up cobra style, and watched us with an unblinking stare. I insisted to the ranger that that wasn't good enough, because the snake would return to the warm macadam as soon as we left. "Move him further into the woods," I commanded. The ranger obliged, and I watched in awe the beauty of the snake as it slithered around rocks and over a log until it disappeared into the safety of the forest.

Eleven

It takes a special kind of passion, of empathy, to make a career of working with sick animals. Dr. P., the veterinarian who euthanized the injured rabbit Steve and I found on the road had the perfect heart for his profession.

His simple office downstairs from the main house did not have a lot of secret back rooms where, in larger practices, technicians disappeared with the animals. Here, the patients and their owners walked down the sidewalk alongside the house and entered into a large single room with the reception area on one side and the surgery on the other.

I would often visit the practice to help Dr. P.'s receptionist, Rachel, with light administrative duties. I loved spending time there and seeing the rapport Dr. P. and Rachel had with the clients...and drinking in the workings of a small veterinary practice.

One evening, Dr. P. and I were alone in the office. A client came in with a Beagle that needed some kind of surgery, and Dr. P. asked me to assist him. This was a first! Being the only "assistant" available to participate hands-on in veterinary surgery! The enormity of this responsibility filled to capacity a dream in my quintessential self. While

I did little except hold the anesthetized dog's leg out of the way, I could again almost taste my desperation to follow a career path in the veterinary field. It seemed so unfair that a small detail like my inability to balance an equation should deny me what I felt in my heart to be my true calling. And to make the evening even more bittersweet, Dr. P. paid me for my assistance just like he would pay a professional vet tech. Ah, but I knew that such payment, day to day, week to week, year after year for doing what I loved most was a dream never to be realized.

The one downside (from my point of view) of Dr. P.'s practice was his refusal to invest in modern gas-type anesthesia. Rather, he chose to anesthetize via injection. Not a problem in and of itself, but much less controllable than gas. Whereas gas can be regulated during surgery, once an anesthetic has been injected into a body, it cannot be removed. To compensate for this limitation, Dr. P. anesthetized his patients so they were "sleeping light," which often meant that the animals could feel what he was doing. I lost count of how many times my heart broke when I heard patients cry out during surgery.

I remember one such operation in particular when a Rottweiler puppy was on the table to be spayed. Being partial to Rottweilers, I stood at the puppy's head while Dr. P. worked on the dog with Rachel's assistance. As the puppy cried and then screamed, I held my face close to her head, stroked her ears and talked to her. Rachel noticed my tears, and I saw her nudge Dr. P. to administer some more anesthetic. He did, and the puppy relaxed and came through the surgery fine. When the puppy awoke, I still stood there holding her head. The puppy reached her face up and licked my face as if to thank me for comforting her during the surgery.

Several months later, I was again with Dr. P. and Rachel in the office when that same Rottweiler, now a large dog, was brought in for routine shots. I sat on the sofa on the waiting room side of the practice as she was brought in, and this big beautiful dog must have remembered me. Even though leashed, she made her way over to me, put her front paws on my shoulders and slobbered me with kisses. I wrapped my arms around the dog's neck and saw the concerned and puzzled looks of Dr. P., Rachel, and the owner as I sat there dwarfed by the Rottie and soaking up the love.

Twelve

Once upon a time when in my early 20s, my boyfriend and I were walking on the side of a curvy four-lane main road. No idea why we were not in my car. Whatever. We rounded a bend and found ourselves before a field that was alive with grasshoppers, and I freaked out. Of course, I did! You remember my stories about the spiders?

My survival instinct kicked in hard and instructed me to run into the middle of the road. Escape from the jumping menaces took precedence over the odds of conversion into a speed bump by cars zooming past at 40-45 MPH.

This story might have had a different ending had John been unable to corral me and yank me back to safety even as I continued to struggle. I'm not a large person, but even a diminutive person in a blind panic can be a handful for someone like John who, when turned sideways, all but disappeared. Maybe his body, too, pumped an extra shot of adrenaline through his system as he struggled to contain me. John's survival instinct, more trustworthy than mine, advised me to close my eyes so he could guide me through the formidable grasshoppers before we both got killed—much like you would blindfold a horse when leading it through fire. I followed his instruction, but I also resisted him as we continued to take one hard-fought step after the other past the field. Unlike a horse, I knew the cloud of grasshoppers was out there even if I couldn't see it, and I believed with all my heart that any minute, one of those things would land on me and send me into cardiac arrest.

What the people passing us in their cars must have thought when they saw the two of us lunging about and zigzagging into and out of the road is anybody's guess. But no one stopped and since the advent of cell phones and YouTube was decades away, we were in no danger of being "caught on camera" and "going viral."

While in the throes of near delirium, I heard the whoop of a siren. A police car with flashing lights had pulled up alongside us, and one of the cops in the car asked us if everything was okay. I remember John's answer like it was yesterday. He indicated the wild-eyed and frantic creature next to him and said with a straight face and in all seriousness, "She's afraid of the grasshoppers."

My memory gets a little fuzzy here but next thing I knew, John and I were sitting in the rear seat of the police cruiser being driven to safety past the grasshopper-infested field. To this day, I wonder if the cop thought I was tripping on LSD; it was *that* era, and it still baffles me that we weren't driven to police headquarters or the nearest hospital for evaluation.

For what it's worth, grasshoppers no longer frighten me. Centipedes give me fits.

Thirteen

So many times, I've noticed how good things happen when I least expect them and when I'm not busy trying to force fate to my own will. In 1985 after I'd sold Flame and soon after Steve and I had moved forward on separate paths, I began working towards my EMT certification at the Fire and Police Academy. A few weeks into my training, I sat in the lecture hall waiting for class to begin and thinking about all the other things I'd rather be doing on a Saturday morning. My mind wandered among daydreams but jerked awake to the present when a would-be clone of the blue-eyed, wavy-haired late country music singer, Eddie Rabbitt, walked into the hall and drove all things EMT clear out of my head. How had I never noticed this guy before? My eyes followed him as he sat down several rows in front of me, and I know I devoted more attention to the back of his head than to whatever the instructor discussed that day. At end of class, the object of my obsession disappeared before I could get to him, but I saw him pull out of the parking lot in a black Trans Am. The following Saturday arrived after what seemed like a month, and I saw the Trans Am when I pulled into the parking lot. I walked into the lecture hall having steeled myself to look for "Eddie" and make eye contact with him, but I was stunned to see him sitting in the front row right behind the sign-in sheets. I managed a brief smile at him with briefer eye contact, and high-tailed it up the stairs to sit with friends from my own squad who were there for a refresher course. Halfway through the lecture, everyone was shuttled into a large room to be assigned permanent partners for practical training. I stood with my other squad members and watched with mingled jitters and delight as "Eddie" walked into the room and stood near our group, and I couldn't believe it when my squad captain paired me with this guy. This guy, Vinny, also there for a refresher course as I learned later, had noticed me as well and had waited until I'd gone into the room so he could see where I went, join my group and have a chance to be my partner. And so it's been for 33 years with my Wookiee (so named after the Star Wars character because of facial fuzziness). For richer, for poorer. In sickness and in health…the whole nine yards, even if without society's official stamp of approval.

I retired from the corporate world nine years ago (2009). And I soon found myself at loose ends, bored out of my skull, and sliding toward depression for want of something productive to do. I spent my days watching *The Young and the Restless* and whatever else I could find on television. While I itched for physical and mental stimulation, I would not/could not motivate myself to budge until it was time to prepare dinner. Bookshelves sagged with unread books. My crafts bin bulged with unfinished needlepoint and crochet projects. The longer I went without some kind of boot to get me off my butt, the more difficult it became to exert any energy beyond what it took to press the remote channel changer so I could watch other people living while I remained a spectator. In retrospect, I might have borrowed a page from *Farenheit 451*.

Little by little, the idea of professional in-house pet sitting formed inside my head. Keeping company with dogs and horses and almost any other type of fuzzy critter had always grounded me, put me in touch with the essence of my soul. But Vinny limits the admission of fur balls in the house to my ferrets. And since Vinny pays the mortgage, it's his call.

Pet sitting on a regular basis, I thought, would provide a win for all parties. Yes? Clients could vacation or attend business meetings away from home with peace of mind knowing their pets were cared for and loved. I would get my fur therapy fix and get paid for doing what I loved. Vinny wouldn't have to listen to me whine about getting a dog. Only one catch: He would get saddled with ferret care when I wasn't home, something he agreed to with little complaint. In truth, a most excellent Wookiee.

Before lethargy could reclaim me, I placed an ad online lauding my virtues and other qualifications and, within days, had landed my first pet-sitting assignment. At last! Something new! Something different! Something to get me out of the house and reengaged in life! But my universe has an earthy sense of humor, and said first assignment after declaring it my business, complete with "Stormie's Joy" business cards and a set fee, almost proved to be my last.

There were two dogs: Barney, a high-energy yellow Lab, recently rescued from somewhere down south, and Molly, a sweet black Lab… and a gerbil that I was warned might die while I was at the house. Happy to say the little guy remained alive and well during my stay.

When walking Barney and Molly the first evening, I noticed that Barney's poop had a reddish tint to it. The sun was setting so I couldn't be sure if the discoloration was a trick of the light or something more insidious. I made a mental note to keep an eye on it.

The next morning when I emerged from the bedroom to grab the dogs' leashes and take them for their first walk of the day, my eyes which had been heavy-lidded from sleep, jerked wide open at the scene that met them in the living room. Blood and bloody stool were everywhere. I felt the room tilt. Barney lay on the floor looking miserable—lackluster eyes, drooping head. I encouraged him to stand and accompany me for a short walk whereupon he pooped more of the bloody mess.

I called the vet as soon as we returned home and after describing Barney's condition, was instructed to bring him in without delay. No argument here. Barney's owner ("Jackie;" I'm ashamed to admit I don't remember her name.) had left her keys and given me permission to use her car whenever and wherever I transported the dogs. The veterinary hospital was located less than ten minutes from the house, and the short trip proved uneventful in terms of Barney getting sick in the car.

The vet, after examining Barney, wanted to keep him the entire day and overnight. He wasn't sure what kind of a "bug" besieged Barney since the dog wasn't from the local area. I told him that I was caring for Barney while the owners were in England. The vet knew Jackie and would treat Barney before Jackie returned to settle the bill, but he thought it best to hold off telling Jackie what was going on until a clear diagnosis could be reached. Hmm. I wasn't too sure about that last. What I was sure about was that on my first pet-sitting assignment, one of the dogs left in my care had developed some kind of a mysterious intestinal thing which, of course, had to be my fault.

I wrestled with the idea of following the vet's suggestion to not notify Jackie. Should I risk ruining their vacation? There would be a huge vet bill. Had the family bonded enough with Barney to lay out that kind of money? Maybe they would rather have him put down. I needed a second opinion so I called Julie, a friend whom I respected and trusted and who owned a yellow Lab for whom I had cared a couple of times as a favor. What would she want me to do if she were away and something happened to Buddy? Would she want to be informed? Julie's response was immediate and emphatic. Yes, absolutely, she would want to know. As Julie pointed out, if I did not inform Barney's owners of the situation, I put myself in the position of making decisions that I neither should have to make nor had a right to make. Thank you, Julie, for highlighting the only right thing to do.

Heeding Julie's excellent counsel, I called Jackie's sister, the emergency contact I'd been given before Jackie left and explained the situation to her. She agreed straight out that Jackie would want to be informed, and she herself would email the details of what was happening with Barney to her. Within a couple of hours, I received an email from Jackie instructing me to take any and all necessary steps to help Barney. Oh good! I could so get on board with that plan of action.

I then turned my attention to the nasty-looking living room, scrubbing the carpet on my hands and knees in an attempt to clean up all the blood. Serious thoughts of ending my fledgling business before it even got off the ground flooded my brain after my efforts at restoring the carpet to its prior condition proved futile. Stubborn dark stains remained. Feeling somewhat nauseated from what could qualify as one of "America's Dirtiest Jobs," I called Vinny in tears and explained the situation to him. He would stop at Home Depot, rent an industrial carpet cleaner, and be over as soon as he could. He then drove forty-five minutes to where I nursed a growing feeling of despair and spent most of the afternoon attempting to clean the carpet. Vinny's efforts, too, resulted in little improvement in the rug's condition.

The vet phoned the next morning to say Barney looked much better. The bug (some long name) appeared to have worked its way out of his system, and Barney could return home but should have no dinner that night. When the vet walked Barney out to me, he did indeed appear to be feeling better with bright eyes and pricked ears, although a quieter and subdued version of himself. During our routine walks that day, Barney produced normal poop, and I tried not to watch his pitiful expression as I ate my own dinner, having left him outside on the deck when I fed Molly.

Two days after Barney's sleepover at the veterinary hospital, he appeared to have returned to his normal high-energy self, and

I thought it safe to venture to the local dog park where Jackie took them. While there, Molly chased, caught, and returned anything that was thrown by me or another dog owner. Such a retriever! Barney tended to be more group oriented and chose to run with a pack. Both dogs had great fun, and I took them to the park from then on almost every day.

One time, I saw several dogs bullying a smaller weaker dog. Barney snarled and jumped into the fray displaying none of his usual playfulness, but rather a viciousness I'd never seen in him. His display of raw aggression scared me, and I pulled him away and took the dogs home wondering what had gotten into Barney.

A similar event happened a few days later when I saw a larger but more submissive dog being attacked by several others. I couldn't tell if the dogs were just roughhousing, but Barney's aggressive behavior toward the less dominant dog was unmistakable. After witnessing such radical changes in Barney's behavior, I ceased taking him to the dog park and opted, instead, for longer walks.

While Barney's sickness left no lingering smell in the house, Jackie and her daughters returned home to a much-stained carpet. Jackie, however, was little concerned saying they planned to replace the carpet soon anyway. She was surprised by my good Barney/bad Barney stories, but her boyfriend said he'd noticed the same behavior when he'd taken the dogs to the park.

An indirect side benefit of caring for Barney and Molly was that the dog park to which I took them was located within fifteen minutes of what had been my grandmother's house. I hadn't seen the house in forty years since my grandmother died but being so close to it when at the park, I had to see it again. I needed to see if the house was still standing, and I needed to reminisce. My happiest childhood memories took place in that house and on that street. So, half scared as to what I would find (that old expression about never being able to go back ran through my mind), and half excited at the chance to relive free and easy childhood joy, I drove over Ridgewood Road and turned left onto Glenside Road to revisit my past and allow hallowed memories of my youth to surface and fill my heart. Much to my delight, the big old house stood there still, well kept, now white with blue shutters instead of pale yellow with green shutters. The screened-in porch that ran the width of the house had been removed, but a charming patio had been installed on the side where once grew a spreading elm before some disease decimated the species. The large copper beech that I used to climb remained front and center on the lawn, although the lowest branch from which I had obtained my foothold into the tree had been sawed off to accommodate a rope-hung swing. Not a bad trade. I felt saddened to see fences that had not existed years ago marking the property lines of many of the houses. But no fences surrounded my grandmother's house, and that made me happy. I drove up the dead-end street recalling the names of almost everyone who lived in those houses long ago. Where were Marylou and Freddy and Stevie and Carolyn and Philippa these days? I remembered the games of hide-and-seek when there were no fences, when all the yards and trees were ours in which to play. And double-Dutch jumping rope in the middle of the street where drivers always moved with caution in anticipation of children engaged in one game or another, heedless of oncoming cars. I turned my car around and headed back down the street feeling fortunate beyond measure to have experienced those carefree childhood days, and wondering if children still played outside on Glenside Road.

The following summer, Jackie called me and asked if I'd be willing to sit for her dogs again. I would have loved to but had committed to another client for one of the weeks Jackie needed me. Jackie said she would get someone else for the week I was busy if I could just come during the second week. Great. But some days later, my first client must have assumed I'd be available for additional days and, without checking first with me, tacked on two or three more days to the time I'd be at her house. My response? Instead of explaining to Nancy that I had a previous commitment and couldn't be there for her the extra days, I notified Jackie that I could only do three days with her dogs instead of the full week for her. A disastrous and stupid mistake on my part, and Jackie made the only reasonable decision she could. She canceled me altogether and never solicited my services again. To this day, I feel ashamed of my actions and hope from the bottom of my heart that I did not ruin Jackie's vacation plans that year with my poor and unprofessional decision making. I now make it a solid practice when dates conflict of always calling the previously booked client to make sure his or her reserved dates are firm. I can be taught! There's that.

Fourteen

I was hesitant, even a little scared, to meet with Mary at her home. Most of my clients live in the country or at least quiet suburbia. Mary lives a block off the main drag in Dover, a small, mostly Hispanic city with all the city trappings: hordes of people on the street, church bells, heavy traffic...and a busy train station. Not used to a city environment, I shrank from the noise and crowds made up of so many people with whom I could not communicate. What little ability I once had to speak Spanish amounted to one semester at college and had been long forgotten.

However, I hate to say "no" to anyone and scheduled the meet and greet with Mary and her two dogs, and which I regretted almost at once when I couldn't find Mary's building at the height of rush hour. I knew her apartment was on the third floor over an office, but all the businesses were closed by the time I got to Dover and found a place to park my car. After about five minutes of walking up and down the street and jumping at shadows, I located Mary's building, but repeated ringing of the doorbell yielded no response. Nervousness increased to low-grade panic. People were starting to watch me, an obvious stranger to the area, with questioning stares (or so I imagined). I returned to my car at a near-run, unlocked the doors, jumped inside, relocked the doors, and called Mary from my cell. She answered before the second ring, and I recounted the last few minutes of my life to her. When I'd finished, she told me I was parked almost in front of her door. Turned out I'd been looking for the wrong address. Things started looking better. I liked Mary on sight, and I loved her dogs, Warren, a sweet timid Bichon, and Sebastian, a feisty Lhasa Apso.

Mary had adopted Sebastian in 2012 from a Pennsylvania shelter to which he had been returned after having been adopted once before. His previous owners, a minister and his family, claimed "it was too expensive to keep him groomed."

Mary found Warren the following February while she walked Sebastian. The little dog was run-

Sebastian

ning down the middle of Warren Street; hence, his name. When Mary first collected Warren, he was shy and defensive and would often bite for about the first year and a half. He learned by degrees to trust people, and like so many other dogs when treated with kindness and patience, developed into the sweetest of animals. And when his curly fur is trimmed short, he looks for all the world like the animal of children's song who "followed her to school one day."

Something about Mary's apartment, too, appealed to me. A kind of melancholy nostalgia stirred memories of my first apartment and my early childhood days when we lived in the city of Orange, New Jersey, a predominantly Italian neighborhood at the time.

Bottom line: I accepted the assignment with Warren and Sebastian. Vinny drove me to the apartment so he could help me carry my luggage up the two flights of stairs, and so I wouldn't have to leave my car in an open lot at night. Any sense of weirdness from not having a car was short-lived as I learned the truth firsthand of what I'd heard people say many times before: "You don't need a car in the city." Bravo's, a small well-stocked grocery store or bodega, was just out the back door and across the parking lot. All sorts of stores lined Main Street half a block away, and the train station was maybe a hundred yards from the front door.

Warren

When left alone for the first time in Mary's apartment, I again felt the wistful sense of familiarity, of déjà vu. Her apartment, which takes up the entire third floor, sits high enough above the street that the clamor below seems far away, even with the windows open. Well, except for the train whistles and the sirens of rescue vehicles. The hallway with its large skylight provides the perfect location in which to sit and delight in the sounds of rain and thunder. It didn't take long before I felt comfortable and mellow cuddling with Warren and Sebastian on the sofa while I watched television or worked on Mary's laptop.

At night, I closed the door separating the living room from the bedroom, inserted my earplugs, and enjoyed uninterrupted sleep. Neither occasional train whistles nor church bells that rang every hour on the hour disturbed me. With Warren curled up on the bed beside me and Sebastian sleeping on the floor next to the bed, I felt cozy and safe.

The first time I descended from my turret to walk the dogs, I discovered a town pulsating with energy. I, with my fair skin, was a clear minority among the olive-skinned, dark-haired Latinos who had to have recognized me as a frankfurter in their paella. But most of the people met my eyes and offered ready smiles as I walked through the center of town, and after seeing me day after day, some would extend verbal greetings and make an effort at simple conversation. In many ways, I found the people of Dover more approachable than those of the Caucasian race to which I belong.

Once when in Bravo's, I waited with my few items in the check-out line behind three or four other people and heard a woman from what looked like a Customer Service counter speak out in Spanish. The woman in front of me on line motioned that I take my things over to the counter for checkout so I didn't have to wait for the other people. It would have been easy for her or any of the others to rush over and get their groceries checked out before me since I had no idea what had been said, and since it's been my experience that whoever is next in line has dibs on a newly opened cashier. I stood at the end of the line and for the shortest length of time, but not one person ahead of me ran over to get their business taken care of a few minutes sooner than anybody else. Lesson learned from a different culture.

As happens with most of my charges, the longer I spent with Warren and Sebastian, the more I got to know them. Warren wants nothing more than to be loved and cuddled. He makes no sound except for a soft whine when he sits on the floor facing me and asks permission to join me on the sofa. Every overture he makes toward me is performed with timidity in hope of the slightest hint of acceptance, be it a smile, a word, a pat on the head—anything but a rebuff. And his response to affection is almost always one of disproportionate appreciation. It's like he tries so hard to be good, almost as if he's afraid of being rebuked and returned to the streets. He doesn't play much but just kind of follows me around wanting to be as close to me as possible. The one time Warren growled at me was when I, in one of my more stupid moments, attempted to retrieve a treat from his mouth that he had trouble handling because it was too big for him. When I tried to take it from him to break it into smaller pieces, he picked it up and walked away from me with his head down in that warning posture that dogs assume when protecting what is theirs. I followed him to one of his beds and reached for it. Low menacing growl reminded me that, sweet as he is, gentle as he is, Warren is still a dog and, at visceral level, a predator who will guard his "prey."

Sebastian, on the other hand, was a bit of a clown who loved to play. He ran around like a wild thing with his tiger hand puppet and dared me to take it from him, only to growl in fun and refuse to give it to me when I tried to grab it. He enjoyed stepping out on his walks but hated to return home. A slow walker under the best of circumstances, as soon as we turned to head back to the apartment, Sebastian would come to a dead stop and refuse to move. Warren would be itching to move on, but I had to almost drag Sebastian to get him walking again. This stop-and-drag routine would repeat itself every few steps until we reached Mary's door. A stranger on the street would have thought I was choking the animal, but Mary told me she had to "insist" that he move as well—unless he saw a moving train while we walked. One leg of our route paralleled the train tracks across the street, and if a train passed us, Sebastian would take off after it as far and as fast as his leash and my arm would allow. But as soon as the train passed, Sebastian would resume his ambling I-can't-go-any-further old-man shuffle. For all his theatrics, he had incredible strength for a small dog— whether chasing trains or refusing to move.

But Warren liked to power strut down the street with his head high in a fair imitation of an Alpha dog. And I enjoyed jetting through town with the little lamb. I'm almost certain that, during our walks, he entertained delusions of ruling the roost. It didn't seem fair that Sebastian should hold him (and me) back. How to avoid ending our walks with a struggle that made us all miserable?

One day, out of desperation, I broke ranks and decided to walk Sebastian around the entire block as I did Warren in the afternoons when I walked each dog by himself. The idea of walking Sebastian through town was a scary proposition. It was embarrassing enough to tow him forward on the side streets. Turned out to be a good move. As I'd hoped might happen by always moving in the same direction around the block, Sebastian never wised up to when we reached the half-way point and headed toward home. He still walked at a slower pace than Warren and I would have preferred, but he ceased presenting the picture of abject misery. And because he stopped planting his feet in resistance, the tug-of-war rituals were no more.

Before being rescued by Mary, Sebastian lived in the parsonage next to a church, which might explain his reaction to the sound of church bells ringing. Whenever we sat outside on the deck and the church bells pealed, Sebastian howled. One balmy July Fourth, the bells rang out patriotic music rather than on-the-hour tolls. I leaned back into the chaise lounge, closed my eyes, felt the warm sun on my face, and listened to the first notes of "America." The rest of the song and all songs that followed were obliterated by Sebastian's letting it all out. I think he just loved the sound of the church bells. Or maybe he hated them.

I received an email from Mary in January 2016 informing me that Sebastian had been diagnosed with diabetes and was receiving insulin twice a day with meals. Would I be okay administering the insulin when I next cared for him in a few months? Of course.

A second email from Mary arrived about a month later. Sebastian had been acting like his old stubborn self that morning until a few hours later and without warning, he appeared lifeless. Mary rushed him to the animal hospital where the vet spent the day running tests on him. Sebastian was placed in intensive care after being diagnosed with having a small blockage in his intestines. The blockage had caused internal bleeding that prohibited surgery, and Mary made the heartbreaking decision to put Sebastian down.

With Sebastian gone, Warren has seemed more like a spirit animal than ever in that if I didn't see him, I wouldn't know he was there. The first couple of days I was last with him, he remained in his bed all day except for meals and walks. Never barked, never complained. He just looked at me with a worried expression on his little face. Maybe with his buddy gone and Mary away, he felt the stirrings of abandonment within him. I wished I could have reassured him that he would never have to worry about being cast away ever again.

Fifteen

Spooky. The first time I cared for two dogs and two cats in Montville—spooky. They and their humans lived in a quiet, over-fifty, affluent development. Well, at the time, an over-fifty affluent development in progress. Less than half a dozen houses had been completed on the Loop, and only about three were occupied during my initial stay. Almost the entire neighborhood, as it stood then, made up one large construction site.

The only sounds Monday through Friday were those of the builders and their machinery. It felt surreal walking the dogs around the trucks and debris through a haze of dust and disconnected sounds. All seemed far away, almost dreamlike, as if I were walking around in some sci-fi movie without direct access to the human race.

The weekend took "spooky" to a new level. With the contractors gone, the silence lay deep and complete, broken only by the distant drone of an occasional plane overhead. And the feeling of being in some distant galaxy reached intense proportions. I remembered a drawing I'd seen years ago in my *Grimm's Fairytales* book of Snow White asleep in a glass coffin, and as I looked through the dining room window onto the deserted street, the comparison of my situation to that picture leapt to mind. I could see out but received no stimuli to which I could respond. I neither heard nor saw a single person, automobile, or even a crow. I thought of stories I'd heard about desensitization chambers and wondered how long it took for a person to go nuts.

Fred and Gene, the two cats, seemed lost downstairs in the large multi-room finished basement where they stayed and where I slept in one of the guest bedrooms. As they moved about on the carpeted floor, my brain overcompensated for the silence and filled in the sound of their "resounding" footsteps.

Oh wait! Did I say that the silence was complete? The high-pitched, almost shrill barking of Buddy the Borzoi and the deep bark of Keno, a Shepherd/Border collie mix, shattered the silence at random intervals much as an air horn from a nearby 18-wheeler jangles the nerves. And because the house had been purchased only months earlier and contained minimal noise-absorbing furniture, fixtures, and freight, the dogs' barking seemed magnified several times over, echoing off the walls and high ceilings. Every sound within the house, the clink of a glass, my footsteps on yet-to-be-carpeted floors, jarred my senses and intensified my feeling of being very small in a very large place.

Saturday and Sunday passed, and a new week began bringing with it the familiar sense that I'd wandered into some kind of parallel universe. But it was better than the tedious deadness I'd endured over the past two days. The return of mirage-like civilization and mirage-like machinery provided welcome relief to my eyes and ears.

Fast-forward three years. The houses have all been built and turned into homes. Even inhabited, tranquility prevails in the neighborhood. The soundproofing within the house is nothing short of absolute. Not once have I heard the sound of the garbage disposal trucks as they make their rounds twice a week in the early morning. I sometimes chance to see another dog-walking human or a car moseying up the street, but the odds are stacked in favor of my being the solitary soul who is out and about. The Loop's ambience that I once viewed as almost creepy, I now find soothing and conducive to deep breathing and writing to the point that when I get to within five minutes of the house, I can feel my biorhythms begin to gear down.

My assignments in Montville, and there have been several, average ten days or longer. Phil and Debbie have raised traveling to an art form and embark on two getaways a year. It makes me happy to know these people who enjoy life, grab it by the horns, and go for it.

About the animals in Montville: Fred (Astaire) and Gene (Kelly), the two cats, so-named in part because of Phil being a dance instructor, are two of the friendliest and most affectionate cats ever. They don't meow, but kind of chitter when they open their mouths and emit raspy squeaks. And both have an insatiable need to watch me pee.

Buddy

Buddy is a 12-year old somewhat loopy and smarter-than-he-pretends Borzoi who could charm the hardest of hearts with his goofiness and sweetness. The world is Buddy's oyster, and he expresses his natural joy often and with ear-splitting exuberance. First thing in the morning when I emerge from downstairs having awakened maybe half an hour earlier, Buddy's "good morning" greetings from behind the gate at the head of the stairs can be a little difficult to take.

His near-constant high-pitched barking, bounding around and kicking up the area rugs while all the time smiling with glee are at once endearing and nerve wracking. His quirkiness extends to mealtimes, which he turns into a comedic act. A finicky eater by nature, I've seen him take a few mouthfuls of food and then lift his head and stare fixedly at his kibble as if waiting for it to twitch. Or, he'll walk a couple of feet away from his bowl, turn his head and look at me, daring me to remove it, only to rush back and put his nose in it as if he were ready to eat the moment I reach for it. His newest trick involves a kind of dining out experience where he takes mouthfuls of kibble at a time, carries it over to the carpet a few feet away, and dumps it where he will sometimes eat it or, more often, just look at it.

Keno is a 13-year old Border Collie-Shepherd mix, one of the most intelligent dogs I've ever met and, unlike Buddy, makes no effort to hide his smarts. He might prove a worthy Scrabble opponent if he could hold the letter tiles in his paws. Less approachable than the gregarious Buddy, Keno acts a little alpha-ish with deep barks and raised hackles when first seeing other dogs, especially at the dog park. But allowed a minute or two to settle down, he joins in the fun without incident.

Keno displays a wolf-like cunning when it comes to getting what he wants. One particular incident stands out in my memory. Each dog had a large peanut-butter-filled bone, which Debbie had left for me to give to them. Keno, dissatisfied with his, headed over to steal Buddy's bone from him, but I recognized his intentions and blocked his way. The marbles rolled around

Keno

in Keno's head for about three seconds, after which he backed away and barked once—that bark that sounds more like a command when he wants a toy I'm holding or when he wants a dog on the other side of the park fence to run with him. Buddy jumped up and loped after Keno who then backtracked and took the unguarded bone while Buddy stood there looking like, "What just happened?" before settling down with the bone Keno had discarded. A little later, I think Buddy tried the same trick that Keno had used on him. Problem: Buddy possesses neither the compelling presence nor commanding bark of Keno. Result: Buddy bombed pitifully and retired to the safe haven of his bed where he played to his own strength and contemplated new comedy routines.

But Keno has been known to have his own less-than-sterling moments, rare as they may be. Once, I had taken the dogs out to the backyard for a potty break with Buddy leashed as usual and Keno unleashed. We had walked over to the far side of the yard so Buddy could inspect some bushes while Keno waited for us by the closed sliding screen door. When Buddy and I returned to where Keno stood, and before I could reach over to slide the door open, Keno turned and walked right into it! I would have laughed out loud had Keno not looked so mortified.

And Buddy, by contrast, has his own moments of brilliance, accidental or not—like, one time, when I gave each of the boys a biscuit. As usual, Keno swallowed his in a gulp. Buddy savored his own biscuit with pieces here and there in front of him and drove Keno to near distraction. When finished, Buddy stood up and waited like a statue while Keno sniffed around and between Buddy's legs for any leftover crumbs. Satisfied that pickins' were nil, Keno settled down with a chew toy, and Buddy raised a front paw and retrieved a fair-sized piece of biscuit! The timing was deliberate; a well-deserved checkmark entered in Buddy's column.

First thing every morning, the dogs and I go for a walk out of the Loop. An easy start to the day. There's a short section, maybe a couple hundred feet or so, after we make our turn out of the Loop onto the main road where no sidewalk exists. One must either walk in the booby-trapped grass with all-but-invisible manholes and dips, or walk in the street where cars zoom past often much faster than the posted 40-MPH speed limit. Since I've learned the location of most of the "mines," I have no problem walking on the grass. But after a snowfall, while the Loop itself is always maintained in pristine condition, the same can't be said of the sidewalks and streets on the main drag.

When enough snow has fallen that the plows have pushed mounds to the side of the road, forcing us to walk in the road, sometimes pretty far out into the road, things get a little dicey. The only mitigating factors might be that fewer cars are on the road, and Buddy who on most days takes forever to find the perfect place to do his business, becomes less picky on cold and wet ground in frigid temperatures.

I had a temporary but intense scare during one morning walk when Keno, who has a history of stomach ulcers, pooped what looked like a lot of blood. Upon closer inspection, it turned out to be some sort of thick, approximately three-inch long piece of red material. Our bodies are amazing works of engineering when it comes to eliminating stuff for which it has no use! When we returned home, I searched for telltale signs of what Keno might have swallowed during the night. The fuzzy red blanket on Debbie and Phil's bed looked to be unharmed. *Ah, but alas!* A hapless once-stuffed monkey was not so lucky. Not only were his squeaker and all his guts gone, but his entire back (red) and most of a leg were also among the missing. I retrieved the monkey, bowed my head, and chucked him without ceremony into the garbage. Keno seemed none the worse for his nighttime binge. He wolfed his breakfast and then, in true Keno fashion, positioned himself a few feet from where Buddy ate and waited with ill-contained patience until Buddy walked away from his bowl leaving whatever spoils to Keno.

Sixteen

got to meet a few people on the Loop during my second or third assignment with Keno and Buddy.

To give the dogs an extra little bit of exercise, I bring them with me when I walk down to the bottom of the Loop to pick up the mail, and I always carry a couple of pooper bags to clean up, just as everyone in the neighborhood cleans up after their dogs. Around 5:00 one afternoon after we'd made our mail run, I heard a knock on the front door. A man I'd never seen stood there. He did not introduce himself but told me he had seen Keno poop on his front lawn, and a turd remained there. It became clear he wanted me to remove it. So, I followed behind him, pooper bag in hand, when he started down the front steps to the street without waiting for me. As I trotted after him, I noticed some folks gathered on the lawn of one of the houses three or four doors down. I wondered if that was my escort's house and if the people had assembled to make sure I did indeed remove the offending turd. My concerns were allayed, however, when one woman whom I assume was the man's wife, laughed and commented on the smallness of the nasty when the man had to search for it in order to point me to it. Had I not found the entire matter so funny, I might have been embarrassed. I removed the dime-sized turd, apologized, and heard the man say something about how he wouldn't have cared except that his young grandchildren were visiting. I didn't learn the man's name until the next day when I met Jen, a lovely woman who lives just across the street from where I was staying. I told her about the incident and expressed concern that I may have caused trouble for Phil and Debbie when they returned from their vacation. Turns out Ray is the Homeowners' Association President in the development and takes his responsibility to heart. But not to worry. He's a good guy and was just looking to maintain the integrity of the Loop.

Seventeen

I drive Buddy and Keno to the park almost every day I'm with them like a good substitute mom. A few years back, I took them for the first time. Snow lay on the ground, which turned out to be a good thing, as I was soon to learn. It was Super Bowl Sunday morning, and I figured no other dogs would be there. Their humans would be shopping for Super Bowl party junk food, or at home preparing for the binge-out, or watching the non-stop game hype on television. Or maybe even at church.

As we neared the entrance to the park, Buddy voiced his enthusiasm and paced back and forth across the back seat around Keno who maintained what would soon be proven to be a deceptive air of calmness as I pulled into the parking lot. I was dismayed to see another dog in the large-dog pen. Oh well. I opened the rear door of my truck and grabbed Buddy's leash, but before I could stop him, Keno jumped out and bolted for the enclosure gate where I was able to grab his leash.

Buddy and Keno are both strong but well-behaved when walking on leash. I pride myself on my ability to control dogs, but I was unprepared for the power with which Buddy and Keno surged forward when adrenaline coursed through their veins at the sight of another dog at the park. The two dogs strained at their leashes with such force that I felt like I was driving horses in a runaway chariot. And when I opened the gate to the large-dog enclosure, both dogs found another gear and sped toward the Rhodesian Ridgeback already in the pen with me dingle-dangling on the other end of their leashes. And I, in a mind-blowing display of either courage or stupidity, fought for control of the dogs—a feat which, by that time, was akin to slowing Secretariat with a halter.

I must have presented quite a sight running full tilt behind the dogs with my arms extended in front of me by the taut leashes. Only when my feet were yanked out from under me and I fell prone into three inches of snow did common sense prevail and permit me to release the leashes. With nothing more than my pride injured, I accepted the assistance of the Ridgeback's owner in regaining my feet. The gentleman was gracious and possessed enough self-control to refrain from bursting into laughter at me as I wiped the snow from my face and arms. We turned our attention to the dogs. Buddy had taken off to the other end of the enclosure, but Keno had run at the Ridgeback that cowered in a corner. By the time I reached Keno and pulled him away, the poor Ridgeback had become so traumatized from Keno's harmless but impressive show of dominance with barking and raised hackles that his owner had difficulty coaxing him out of the enclosure and into his car. It bears noting here that Keno and Fenway have since become friends, and Fred is one of the nicest gentlemen you'd ever want to meet.

I hung around the dog park a while longer to calm my nerves, slow my heart rate, and thank my lucky stars for the snow that had cushioned my fall against what would have been gravel on a warmer day. And my prayers for no other dog(s) to arrive while I remained at the park were granted by a most benevolent God. Since my baptism by fire that Sunday, I've mastered the art of entering the dog park with minimal chaos.

I learned early on to always back up against something solid in the park when Buddy stretches out and runs. It's a beautiful sight to see this klutzy animal race with abandon and turn on a dime while barking with glee the entire time. But he doesn't always see that dime and plows right into whatever is in his path. Keno is quick enough most times to get out of the way of the Buddy juggernaut. But more than once, I've seen Buddy career around a corner and bowl Keno over. One morning, the obstruction was the park bench on which I sat. Buddy ran into it full tilt and, without breaking stride, turned away from it and continued his gallop to nowhere. He doesn't sweat the small stuff!

Those of us who know and love Buddy have enjoyed several laughs at his apparent goofiness and lack of coordination. But a few months ago, a veterinarian discovered that Buddy's penchant for walking or running into things is the result of impaired peripheral vision. I noticed the last time I was with him that when he dropped a dog biscuit between his front paws, he couldn't find it. I had to pick it up and hand it to him again. Also, when Buddy hears the garage door open, he runs upstairs to a window that overlooks the driveway so he can watch to see if the car continues onto the road and out of sight, or if I get out of the car which signifies I'll be coming back inside to maybe take him to the park. The last time I left, however, I looked up at the window. Buddy was there, but it appeared that he couldn't see my truck. He kept cocking his head slightly as if trying to focus. Poor baby. As of the time of this writing, no treatment is known that might improve or prevent possible further deterioration of his eyesight. However, Buddy's less-than-perfect vision fails to hamper his zest for life. He continues to greet every person, animal and experience with an open and joyful heart.

Sometimes, for whatever reason, we see no one at the park for days on end. Once, after being the solitary inhabitants for almost a week, we had company on the last hot summer day of my assignment: a large German Shepherd that I'd never seen before. When the dog and his owner entered the enclosure, Keno neither barked nor raised his hackles, as he always does when another dog arrives. He walked over to Jake (as the dog was called), engaged in a mutual sniff and walked away. I attribute this break from the norm to the fact that Keno is part German Shepherd.

Shepherds have a documented and legendary communication system and instinctive respect for one another. I'd seen this phenomenon firsthand with Kona, a German Shepherd for which I've cared. Kona was off the wall when she was younger and unmanageable on a leash. She wasn't aggressive—just short on attention span and, therefore, wanting to chase or play with anything, anyone or any dog that crossed her path. One morning while walking Kona in a nearby park, we met an older German Shepherd, Riley. Kona dropped to the ground and crawled up to Riley in total submission. The two dogs engaged in a Shepherd one-on-one, but whenever Kona got too rambunctious, Riley reprimanded her with a growl, and Kona backed down at once. Any passerby who might have seen Kona and me during the remainder of our walk would have thought Kona had graduated puppy obedience school with honors.

Back in the dog park with Keno and Buddy, Jake didn't take to Buddy at all. Growled every time Buddy approached him. Buddy's reaction to Jake's rebukes was laughable. He didn't understand why Jake didn't like him. This was a first for Buddy. The let's-be-friends approach failing, I watched Buddy change tactics and make a game of it, coming just close enough to Jake to annoy him and then dancing away when Jake growled. Buddy's shenanigans continued for several minutes until I decided it was time to leave. Keno, meanwhile, had watched the scene from where he lay in the shade of a large tree.

Dog parks attract as many different kinds of people as they do breeds of dogs. The park to which I take Buddy and Keno is no exception.

Like most dog parks, it has three enclosures: a holding pen or common area (where dogs are brought to get acquainted with others through the fences of the specific enclosures), a small-dog pen (for small dogs only), and a large-dog pen (for all dogs at the discretion of the owners).

I arrived one morning with Buddy and Keno and found the large-dog enclosure jumping with canine activity, including a Dachshund among the larger dogs. All the owners and dogs appeared to know each other, and when Keno, Buddy and I arrived, the dogs ran to the fence to greet us in typical frenzied fashion. The Dachshund alone demonstrated clear aggression toward Keno, and Keno reciprocated in kind. I asked the dog's owner to please move her dog to the small-dog enclosure so I could bring my dogs in. She refused saying the large-dog pen was for all dogs, and since Keno was the problem, I should put him in the small-dog enclosure. I reminded her that large dogs were not allowed in that pen, to which she in essence responded "too bad." Frustration mounted, and I called her attention to the interaction between Keno and her dog. Both were snarling with their teeth bared and hackles raised, and Keno was digging like a thing possessed to get through or under the fence. If Keno were to get in, the Dachshund would be dead meat. After some more unpleasantness and threats, I'd had enough and decided to call this woman's bluff, saying "Fine. We're coming in." And I moved to open the outside gate to the holding area. The crazed look in my eyes may have convinced the woman I meant what I said as she regained her sanity and brought her dog to the other pen. I felt like a heel about the entire altercation. The dogs had, in fact, all gotten along well before I arrived with Keno, but I knew he would be fine with the other dogs. And Buddy, well Buddy would make friends as easily with a Mastiff as he would a Chihuahua.

The next day when we arrived at the park, the same group of people and dogs were there. I watched with a twinge of mingled guilt and relief as the woman with the Dachshund wasted no time in taking her dog to the small-dog enclosure. Bad blood nauseates me, and I will go out of my way to avoid it if I can or make things right as soon as possible. After releasing Buddy and Keno into the pen with the large dogs, I walked over to the small-dog enclosure to meet the woman and her Dachshund. Bosco was a love, and Jolene seemed friendly enough, if somewhat guarded. Upon learning I was the pet sitter for Buddy and Keno, she requested one of my cards. I began walking toward my car to retrieve one for her, but that little voice inside me, that same voice that almost never steers me wrong, warned against sharing my information with Jolene. Despite her outward amiability, she might harbor some lingering resentment toward me for separating her from her friends, and she might seek retaliation by complaining to the park police that I had brought an "aggressive" dog to the park. So, after reaching my car and making a show of looking for my cards, I returned and told Jolene I didn't have any cards with me. At the time of this writing, two years later, I haven't seen Jolene and Bosco again.

It's clear that Keno doesn't like most small dogs, but Willy, a Pekinese, is often there with his owner, Betty, at the same time we are. I can't tell if Keno and Willy have a love/hate relationship or if Willy just enjoys teasing Keno and the other large dogs. But as soon as Willy and Keno see each other, regardless of who arrives first, they are both at the adjoining fence between the large- and small-dog enclosures. Then begins a streaking up and down the length of the fence until Willy loses interest, leaving Keno exhausted but standing by the fence issuing staccato-like barks commanding and encouraging Willy to return to the fence and run with him. Sometimes, as many as five or six large dogs all run the fence together looking very much like a pack of wolves. It's an incredible sight, almost scary, as the dogs' instinctive

predatory behavior appears to surface. Willy runs like greased lightning and must realize that he can give the larger dogs a run for their
money and do so in safety while offering himself up as untouchable
prey. Fun to watch.

And then there was the time we arrived at the park one swel-
tering morning and saw two young women already there with their
large dogs. Some smaller dogs were in the other enclosure. I'd never
seen either of these women or their dogs who lay in the shade panting
while their owners busied themselves with their cell phones, oblivious
to life going on around them. At some point, I saw one of the smaller
dogs being led out to the common area for a bowl of water. While the
smaller dog was in the holding pen, one of the two women from our
enclosure got up and walked to the gate, cell phone to ear, presumably
to get some water for the larger dogs. She left the gate open between
the holding pen and our enclosure despite the presence of the smaller dog. Unhappy with this arrangement when Buddy, Keno and the
other two large dogs had congregated at the open gate, I walked over
to corral Buddy and Keno and then watched in disbelief as cell phone
girl continued to walk out of the park, leaving the gate to the parking
lot open as well. One of the dogs ran past her into the parking lot and
snapped the girl back to the real world, causing her to stop and gape
in dumb confusion. The other woman from our enclosure ran to collect the escaped dog that was headed toward the 40 MPH road on the
other side of the lot. Keno, too, had walked out but had not moved
into the parking lot and responded straight away when I called him.
Good dog! Again, while I don't like conflict, I also don't suffer well
the degree of carelessness and stupidity evidenced by the woman who
had left the gates open, and I took the opportunity to tell her (in the
most civil of tones, all things considered) that she needed to be more
responsible with the animals and close the gates. Her immediate response: "It wasn't my fault. Someone else left the gate open." What
could I say to that level of denial and refusal of accountability after I'd
just watched the scene unfold with my own eyes? Civility took flight,

but I turned and walked away, choosing deep calming breaths over the much-too-difficult-to-resist alternative of assault.

The majority of people who frequent the park the same time that I do know me. For the most part, all the dog owners are good natured and attentive to their dog(s). They include me in conversation. They notice when their charges do their business, and they clean it up after them. It irks all of us that some people, maybe when at the park alone, do not clean up after their dogs. Perhaps the recent installation of cameras will keep people honest.

Per Debbie's instructions early on, I keep Keno leashed for a minute or two when we arrive at the park if there are other large dogs already there or when others arrive. Not that a problem would ensue, but Keno sometimes gets excited and goes into his alpha dog routine which could frighten some dogs or instigate trouble with a more assertive dog. Keeping him leashed for a short time gives him a chance to settle before he gets down to the business of pooping, butt sniffing, playing, or chasing Willy if the Pekinese happens to be there. The other dog owners know Keno and appreciate that I engage in this practice... that is, until one morning when Buddy, Keno and I were at the park alone, except for one woman and her dog in the small-dog enclosure. Another woman arrived and walked her Golden Retriever around the outside of the enclosure, uncertain about Keno who barked and led me around the fence after I'd leashed him when I saw her arrive.

Then a man whom I'd never seen arrived with two more dogs who barked when brought into the "holding pen." This man demanded that I unleash Keno. I refused, explaining to him over the din of the barking my standard procedure. He didn't want to hear it and said he wouldn't bring his dogs into the enclosure while I had my dog leashed. He emphasized that he was a trainer and that I knew nothing about dogs. By this time, the woman and Golden Retriever were standing nearby as were the woman from the small-dog enclosure and Buddy, and the dogs were all hysterical. It was crazy. I moved Keno away from the gate, and the man continued to demand that I unleash my dog. At one point, he threatened to call the police. Since I was the new kid on the block, the outsider, and figured all these people knew each other, and since no one except this man was saying anything one way or the other, I began to think I should listen to him—if for no other reason than I was feeling embarrassed for having caused this scene. I unleashed Keno, who immediately ran to the gate. The man then unleashed his own dogs in the holding pen, the woman unleashed her Golden in the pen, the woman with the small dog left the park, and everyone quieted down. The man continued his rudeness after releasing his dogs into the large-dog enclosure and made a point of ignoring me while talking to the Golden's owner loud enough for me to hear him go on about my ineptitude with dogs. After listening to him rant for more than ten minutes, I approached him and asked him why he hadn't told me he was going to leave his dogs in the holding pen until the dogs simmered down rather than being obnoxious from the moment he'd arrived. I told him I'd have taken Keno off the leash without question had I understood his plans. He didn't answer me except to say that I was wrong to leash Keno because it made dogs aggressive. He didn't want to hear that I was following instructions from his owners and that there had been no problem in the past with my containing Keno for a few minutes. Instead, he repeated that he was a trainer and he knew dogs. I on the other hand knew nothing and received the very clear impression that he considered my brain incapable of formulating any thought more complicated than "red light, stop; green light, go."

When I recounted the incident next day to some of the regulars, they told me that "Dan" usually came to the park later in the day. His default personality was offensive and inconsiderate toward women, and the fact that I had stood up to him had driven him into conniptions. And oh, by the way, the only dogs Dan trained were his own. I guess word got around about the confrontation between Dan and me because from then on, anytime Dan's name came up in conversation, no matter with whom, it was always accompanied by knowing smiles and the shaking of heads.

That was the last time I saw Dan, but by my next assignment with Buddy and Keno, dog park rules had been posted on the fence. They included the requirement that all dogs be unleashed in the holding pen for a couple of minutes before joining other dogs in their respective enclosures. A good idea, but nothing about the extension of common courtesy and respect toward other owners.

Eighteen

People sometimes demonstrate the infinite lengths they will go to prove the depth of their heartlessness and stupidity.

Case in point: Once, while driving on Waterloo Road, a quiet wooded street near our house, and reveling in gorgeous spring-like weather, I watched in disbelief and horror as the young driver of a late-model convertible in front of me sped up and plowed through a brace of ducks that ambled across the road. The ducks scattered and flew out of harm's way, except for one that sustained injury and flopped around on the ground. I heard the kids' maniacal laughter as they drove away after shattering with brutal savageness an otherwise idyllic moment in the woods.

While I grasped for the driver's motivation for such wanton violence against nature, I got out of my car intending to capture the wounded duck and take it to a veterinarian. The sought-for motivation eluded me and left me wondering instead about the twisted brain works of some people. The duck meanwhile, in response to my efforts to help it, half-ran/half-flew out of my reach and into the woods where I couldn't catch it. Maybe it had been stunned, but not hurt.

An unbidden memory came to mind of an incident from several years back when I collected a crow that had flown into the grill of my tiny two-seater Fiat 850 and lay unconscious on the ground. I had been on my way to work at the time, but I couldn't leave the scene of an accident, even if the other party involved was a bird. So, after retrieving the crow and putting it on the passenger side of the floor, I continued my drive and kept a lookout for a gas station or diner where I might find a phone book and locate the nearest vet. The confounded bird, without warning, regained consciousness and began hopping around on the floor. I was grateful for the gear shift and hump that divided my side of the car from that of the bird, but visions of it clearing the hump and getting caught in the pedals or, worse, flying around inside the car, gave me a whopping case of the willies. I turned off the main road at my first chance and, wonder of wonders, came to a large field. Perfect! I stopped the car, reached over and opened the passenger side door and waited for the crow to exit. What it did instead was jump onto the saddle, turn around, look me straight in the eye, and issue a defiant screech. Well, maybe it was a screech of gratitude. Anyway, it then dropped out of the car and ran up the field. I was concerned that it didn't fly away, but I've heard that crows are super smart. Maybe it still felt a little loopy and knew better than to take flight until its head cleared.

Whether that duck on Waterloo Road was injured or just stunned, I am certain that the image of the car tearing into the ducks will haunt me forever. It constituted a repugnant and malicious act that cannot be explained away with the feeble excuse of driver distraction. No accidental roadkill here. I would curse the driver of that convertible but for remembering that vengeance is not mine. Call it karma. Call it fate. Call it Judgment. At the end of the day, no one gets away with anything. Rev. 22:12.

Nineteen

I want to see a bear. Almost everyone I know has seen at least one, some more than one on multiple occasions. Bears have wandered through our own backyard as caught by motion-sensitive cameras, but they always visit when I'm not looking even though the time on the video indicates I was home when the camera activated. One time, Vinny called me from the bottom of our street a few hundred yards away to tell me he'd just seen a bear, a big one, heading in the direction of our house. I ran from window to window hoping to catch a glimpse of it, but said bear must have veered off before it got to our house. Figures!

Several clients have pretty much "guaranteed" that I will see a bear, especially on trash night. So far, nada. In four years of pet-sitting in wooded, bear-friendly areas, I have seen not one bear. However, I *may* have come within close proximity to a bear, even if I didn't see it.

A year before the possible encounter, my friend Cathleen asked if I would accompany her to retrieve an eight-week old German Shepherd fur ball named Kona from her breeder in upstate New York. Yes! Thank you! I'd known Cathleen had selected a puppy, but I hadn't dreamed she'd ask me to help bring it home. I could think of no a greater privilege than that "favor" requested of me by Cathleen. Kona was a sweetheart and traveled well, sleeping in her crate for most of the ride home and riding in my lap the last half hour or so. I fell in love with her and looked forward to the time when Cathleen might call upon me to care for Kona when the family went away. The opportunity presented itself late the following summer when Kona was not quite two years old.

At the rear of Mark and Cathleen's deep sweeping backyard is a small tree-splattered woods with a natural path on which Kona loves to walk when not being exercised in the local park. One afternoon, I leashed Kona for a trek into said woods and, upon sliding open the glass door to the deck, heard several dogs barking in the distance. I'd never heard even one dog bark in that serene neighborhood.

I poked my head out, looked around, saw nothing, and stepped outside with Kona. Kona, too, acted antsy. Rather than straining at the leash in her eagerness to scope out the woods for the umptieth time, she walked up the long gentle grade of lawn toward the trees lifting each foot deliberately and placing it down with care as if tiptoe-ing for fear of making the grass creak. She stopped short at the edge of the woods with a well-tucked tail and the rest of her body on high alert—almost quivering. Standing stock still with eyes straight ahead and ears pricked, Kona would have wowed the judges at an AKC dog show. But except for the sound of the barking dogs, I heard nothing unusual. If demons lurked along the shaded path before us, they kept their secret well.

I again looked around, saw nothing, and urged Kona into the woods. Kona left no doubt about her qualms at being among the trees and, once surrounded by them, tried to bolt through them—a clear departure from her normal default mode of stopping to smell every rock, chew every stick, or leap to chase every butterfly.

Her behavior unnerved me, transforming the tranquil setting into something almost malevolent. The stillness of the woods took on a haunted quality, and the cool shade raised goosebumps on my arms. The dogs' barking, while fainter now, continued. I remember wondering why I, who made a practice of respecting a dog's instincts, chose to discount Kona's uneasiness and attribute it to something no more dire than the barking dogs.

Bright sunshine ahead of us signaled an end to the clingy gloom. But just as we were about to step into the light with Kona still surging at the leash, a loud, deep, prolonged growl broke the silence. Kona and I froze on the spot. That disembodied threat sounded close!

Yet again, I looked around and saw nothing, but this time I ran with Kona back to the house. No urging necessary. This "Hound of the Baskervilles" incident failed to temper my desire to see a bear, but it did cause me to add a caveat to my "desperately wanting to see a bear:" I want to see it before it sees me.

Twenty

I hate hearing about dog fighting (and cockfighting, too, for that matter) and wish with all my heart that every one of the sickos who promotes such bloodletting "sport" would be caught and imprisoned. On the flip side, I love the folks who rescue dogs from that brutal existence, and I've had the joy and privilege of caring for several such fortunate dogs who have been given a second lease on life. Such treasures!

One such dog, a Staffordshire Terrier named Jada, is a Katrina rescue. Her owners, David and Susan, found Jada online during a Puptoberfest Eleventh Hour Rescue fundraiser. When they took possession of Jada, then five years old, they were informed that a large lump on her left flank was "just a fatty tumor." It turned out to be a stage four cancer. David and Susan had the tumor removed at their own expense. More lumps have since appeared, including a large one on Jada's tail, which the vet feels is too close to her spine to risk removal. Jada is now about twelve years old and appears to be happy and comfortable despite another lump on her hind leg that causes her difficulty in managing stairs. The deep scars on her flanks and the extreme shortness of her ears, coupled with her love for people and aggression toward all other dogs, indicate that she must have been used as a bait dog, if not a competitor in dog fights while down South.

David and Susan are two of the kindest and most mellow people I've ever met and have undergone and survived many trials, physically, financially and emotionally. Given their circumstances, who *wouldn't* be challenged in their ability to cope with the day-to-day clutter of life? The entire family, including David and Susan's young son Matthew, loves Jada to death, but with so many demands on her time, Susan finds it difficult to walk Jada as often as would be healthy for the dog. So, Jada has grown soft and flabby—a well-loved canine couch potato.

Jada

I walked Jada twice a day those times when she was left in my care, and as weather permitted, I took her to a nearby park and walked her through the woods. Happy girl. She pooped so often that I admonished Susan to make time to walk Jada, who had to have been in some discomfort given the pressure on her bowels. I know Susan took my words to heart and tried to comply with my recommendation.

In addition to scads of distractions in their lives, David and Susan volunteered to have a Centenary College international student from China live with them instead of in the dorm. The arrangement provided an opportunity to interact with and learn about someone from another culture. The student David and Susan took into their modest home paid them a nominal monthly fee and remained with them for almost 18 months.

Once, when the student would be away, I arrived at the house to begin a Jada-care assignment. I found the key in the predetermined location and let myself in through the back door. As with most of my gigs, I plan my arrival for after the owners have gone, and my departure before they return to minimize confusion. Susan had told me her boarder would be gone by the time I arrived.

She was indeed gone, but the scene that greeted me as soon as I walked into the kitchen reminded me in vivid technicolor of the often sloppy and unthinking nature of teenagers. The kitchen resembled that which might be found in a poorly run restaurant. Dirty dishes filled the sink, half-filled pots and pans sat on the filthy stove, and worst of all, partially eaten soft-shelled crabs remained on plates at the table. I fumed and paced (in silence, I think) while condemning the student and wondering how Susan could put up with this lack of consideration, in addition to the other demands on her time. I also wondered where I would find the ambition to even begin to clean the kitchen.

The crabs, in particular, bothered me. They scared me and disgusted me, and they made me sad. I never eat anything that looks like an animal. When I order lobster tail at a restaurant, I always ask for it without the shell. One time, a waiter laughed at me and said, "So you want lobster salad." Another time, when I'd ordered seafood paella, I removed the lid from the crock and saw a big lobster tail floating on top. Vinny, my hero, removed it and hid it under his napkin while I closed my eyes.

But those half-eaten crabs in Susan's kitchen with their helpless claws, and as I interpreted them, accusing beady eyes, chilled me to the bone. I was afraid to even approach the plates, let alone move them, so I resorted to that age-old means of dealing with unpleasant situations. I forced it out of my mind, walked away from the kitchen and up the stairs with my bags.

While unpacking, I heard the backdoor slam and the sound of voices from the kitchen. I crept downstairs and saw to my amazement and immeasurable relief the student and her friend beginning to clear the kitchen. The girls were polite and apologetic for the mess when they saw me standing in the doorway, and as I watched the plates with those fearsome crabs being scraped into the garbage and out of sight, I felt like I'd been delivered from something far worse than hard labor. And I remember the grace demonstrated by the girls when I asked them to please take the garbage bag outside to the trash because I didn't want to see the crabs when I lifted the lid of the kitchen can to throw it all away.

Another incident that remains crystal clear in my memory with Jada occurred during an afternoon walk over Labor Day. I knew the quiet neighborhood well, having cared for Jada several times. But that particular afternoon as we walked by one familiar yard, two large pit bulls, each tethered to a cinderblock, saw us and ran toward us dragging the concrete weights behind them like they were mere nuisances. Both dogs leapt upon Jada, who tried to defend herself while I held her leash. Several people, some of whom I presumed owned the pit bulls, sat on the deck with their cocktails and laughed in raucous amusement. I heard one woman say in amazement, "They're pulling the cinderblocks!" *Duh!* Like a small piece of cement would hinder a charging pit bull. I, meanwhile, bellowed for someone to get the dogs off Jada. After what seemed like an eternity, two men strolled over to us like they were planning to look at prize roses in a garden, and restrained the dogs. Neither man apologized for the attack, and neither showed the least bit of concern for Jada or me. I saw no obvious injury to Jada, and we continued walking the last block toward home while my thumping heart gradually returned to a rate somewhat akin to normal. But my anger simmered at the nonchalance and gross negligence of the pit bulls' owners.

I notified David and Susan of the attack as soon as we returned to the house and assured them there didn't appear to be serious, if any, harm done. But I told them I'd seen a car with Georgia license plates parked on the street just outside the house where the attack happened. Since I'd never seen the pit bulls before in all the times I'd walked Jada, and since it was a holiday, I figured the dogs must have belonged to the out-of-staters. David and Susan would return home the next day, and I requested that they call me after examining Jada for themselves.

When Susan called, she told me she'd found a small puncture wound on Jada's face. I encouraged Susan to take the dog to the vet and sue the owners of the two pit bulls for the cost of the initial exam, any medications the vet might prescribe, and any follow-up visits. When Susan expressed hesitancy to approach the people, I offered to go for her. In the 24 hours since the incident, I had researched canine law and learned that if David and Susan wanted to sue, it would be a slam dunk in their favor. In fact, I also learned that if a dog owner has a dog tethered and fenced, even with a visible fence, but that dog somehow gets loose and does injury to property, a person or another animal, the owner is still liable for damages. For whatever reason, be it their already full plates or their innate gentle and forgiving person- alities, David and Susan chose to avoid conflict and, despite my as- surances and encouragement, refused to pursue the matter and opted instead to absorb the cost of Jada's medical treatment themselves.

Jada found her forever home through deliberate actions on the part of David and Susan. Some animals, however, enter our lives through what would appear to be chance and mutual good fortune. But I don't believe in chance. I believe that animals, like people, who come into our lives do so by Sovereign Design.

While driving home one night, Lou, another client of mine, saw what he thought was a fox on the side of the road. He stopped to look with the intent of helping whatever it was if possible. Turned out to be a dog, a starving Jack Russell Terrier. Lou, who already owned a Spitz and a Norwegian Elkhound, opened the car door, and the little dog jumped in without hesitation. When he arrived home with the dog in his arms, Lou figured his wife, a nurse who'd worked three consecu- tive nights would be less than thrilled with the addition of a third dog. But when she saw the dog, Andrea understood and believed that Lou had done the right thing by bringing the animal home. She loved Allie (as the dog came to be called) at first sight but exhaustion drove her to bed where she fell asleep within minutes. Meanwhile, Lou bathed Allie and removed more than 50 fleas from her, after which he fed her and put her at the foot of their bed. By the time he returned to the bedroom a few minutes later, he saw that Allie had moved up the bed to his pillow and was fast asleep. So Lou did what any animal-loving person would do; he slept somewhere else.

A visit to the vet confirmed that Allie's many scars most likely resulted from her being used as a bait dog in fights. She was maybe three years old when Lou found her and had already had at least one litter of puppies.

While I would exercise her more and feed her less to render her several pounds lighter, Allie is a gentle and happy dog, and she is loved by all who meet her.

Allie and Jada exemplify the resilience of so many animals that have endured horrific cruelty at the hands of humans. Both dogs have a deep-seated trust in most people, believing them to be good and compassionate, and both dogs are loving and affectionate toward anyone who is kind to them.

Twenty-one

Life with ferrets—akin to life with a toddler, and not for the faint of heart. They require pretty much uninterrupted attention when not in their cage, and it's always a scary thing when they're too quiet for too long. They steal things, and they don't tell you where they've hidden them. They use their out-of-cage litter box only on rare and special occasions. They fit themselves into and under things of such small size as to defy all spatial laws. I have owned many ferrets over the past 30 years, some of which have been very smart and others which have gazed upon the bell curve for ferret intelligence from afar. But each animal has been special and unique unto itself, and each has given me much joy and provided hours of comic relief.

After many years of being at a severe disadvantage when it came to dealing with ferret wiles, this mere mortal managed one small step toward some semblance of control over the adorable mini hellions. I was well into my much-deserved title of "local ferret lady" by the time I compiled a list of four never-fail "sound-tricks" to lure the critter from wherever it might be hiding when it knows (and a ferret does know!) it's done something mommy doesn't like. 1. A squeaky toy beats all. Most ferrets I've known will stand their ground even against the dreaded running vacuum cleaner for a chance to sink their teeth into the squeaky. 2. The sound of me walking down the stairs where the man cave, laundry room, and storage room are closed to ferrets. When they hear someone walking downstairs, they will almost always come out from wherever they may be in hopes of slipping into one of those rooms as soon as a door opens. 3. The sound of *any* door opening (closet, refrigerator, shower door, etc.). Ferrets, by instinct, know that behind every closed door lies the possibility of unexplored treasure and an opportunity for demolition—objects to drag off of shelves, boxes in which to burrow, materials to chew. 4. The sound of me clucking for squirrels from the dining room window. Widget, in particular, materialized at my feet within seconds begging for a peanut when she knew I was feeding the squirrels. I could pat myself on the back for having mapped out these ferret-manipulating strategies, but the sad truth is that I spent a ridiculous amount of energy and time trying to figure how to outthink a ferret. When all is said and done, they smile ferret smiles at me and snicker ferret snickers behind my back, and know beyond a shadow of a doubt that I have no clue how to become Alpha Ferret.

Late October 2013, an early-season blizzard in New Jersey canceled Halloween for the second year in a row; super storm Sandy had devastated major sections of the east coast the previous year. I was on assignment during the blizzard and had used flashlights and candles to navigate around the house when we lost power. The next day, power having been restored, I ran the dishwasher and laundered the bed linens and towels in anticipation of my clients returning home a few hours later.

Vinny, too, had lost power at home and had connected our portable generator so that he had some light and heat through the use of a liquid propane space heater. He brought my ferrets, Bounce and Pogo, into the bedroom with him so they would be warm. The next morning while I returned my clients' house to presentable condition, a distraught Vinny called to tell me that Bounce had died overnight. This

Bounce

sad news came as a shock to me. Bounce had been healthy a week ago when I left for my assignment. All I could think and hope was that she died from carbon monoxide poisoning, an easy death. Pogo was a much larger ferret. Maybe the gas hadn't reached toxic levels in his blood. Before I returned home, Vinny did as I asked and dug through the snow, hacked through the not-quite-frozen ground, and buried Bounce in the backyard where my other ferrets had been laid to rest. Bounce was the first ferret I'd owned that I did not need to put to sleep as a result of some form of cancer. And she was the first ferret who died without me being with him or her.

While wheeling my Nissan Xterra home later that morning on plowed but still patchy snow-covered roads, a driver in a black SUV came up behind me and remained close enough behind me for several miles that, at times, I could see no more than the car's grill in my rear-view mirror. The cars in front of me on the two-lane road maintained close to the posted speed limit of 45-50 MPH, and I kept up with them while maintaining a safe distance between them and me—to the obvious displeasure of the Einstein behind me. I half-expected him to try and pass me, despite the double lines on the highway and the slick road conditions. As we approached the malls of Mansfield, the speed limit dropped to 35 MPH, and a red traffic light mandated that we stop. The cars in front of me stopped. I stopped. The SUV behind me did not. And since I'd heard too many stories about how wackos cause deliberate "accidents" and then inflict bad things upon the "victim" when he/she gets out of the car to check for damage, I locked my doors and waited for someone to call 911. A few minutes later, the driver of the SUV got out of his car, made a show of surveying both our cars, and approached the driver side of my car. I cracked my window. Would I like to move my car through the light and off the road? No, I think not. Will wait for police who arrived soon after. I watched from my car as one officer talked to the other driver and then came up to my window with a story, the likes of which I couldn't believe. The driver of the SUV who had done everything in his power for the last 20 minutes to cause a wreck on slushy roads at 50 MPH turned out to be an off-duty cop and, according to the officer standing at my window, had sneezed and been unable to stop in time at the light. Are you kidding me? The audacity with which that driver spouted such a bald-faced lie and the ease with which the police accepted it, staggered my senses. Had I not been so upset about losing Bounce and so rattled from having dealt with the nut case driving behind me, I'd have vaulted from my car, gotten in that driver's face and named him for what he was: a liar hiding behind the fact that he was a cop. Instead, I continued my ride home and contented myself with the belief that what goes

Pogo

around, comes around. As an aside, I support our men in blue one hundred percent. But I realize that as in any other field, there are the occasional few individuals who would besmirch the integrity of any profession.

With Bounce gone, Pogo looked and acted so sad. Ferrets are social animals, and I knew I had to get a friend for him. Vinny made the mistake of sending me to the pet store by myself and, as a result, I brought home two baby ferrets, Gizmo and Widget. Three ferrets were in the tub at the store, and I would have bought all three had I had enough money with me. Such a difficult decision to make about which one to leave behind. Because the ferret babies had just arrived the day before, the folks at the store were unwilling to make a multiple-critter deal with me. So I bought the beautiful cream-colored Widget and the affectionate Gizmo, hoping the remaining little one would find a good home soon.

When Pogo, Gizmo and Widget were out of their cage for their daily run-of-the-house exercise, any observer could see the roles each played in their group dynamic. Gizmo was the "muscle" of the trio, willing and able to leap chairs and coffee tables in a single bound to get at something he shouldn't. Within a month of bringing him home, the not-quite-four-month-old Gizmo, the sweet-faced and fetching Gizmo whose mask made him look like a little bat, figured out how to climb onto the living room sofa, leap nearly three feet across to the coffee table and excavate my philodendron from its planter. And all because I didn't think and turned my focus to something other than him. Sometime later, he scaled a dining room chair and pulled himself onto the table where he dismantled and dragged to the floor most of a Bev Doolittle jigsaw puzzle that Vinny and I had labored over for weeks.

Widget (left) and Gizmo (right)

Pogo fit the "stooge" or "decoy" role to perfection, always sweet and appearing to be clueless as to what was happening around him. What he lacked in ferret brains, he made up for in charm by being the perfect lap ferret. As such, Pogo could distract me with no sweat from his miscreant cohorts.

Widget, atop the ferret bell curve, called the shots while maintaining an aloof and innocent demeanor as mischief erupted around her. She was lightning fast and earned the nickname, "Little Silver Streak." If playing on the far side of the living room, she saw me on the other side of the room heading downstairs, she'd give me half a flight lead time and then, defying every law of physics, would race past me and wait for me at the closed doors by the time I got there. I had to then often perform the crazy acrobatic maneuvers of opening the laundry room door just wide enough to place my foot crosswise between the door and the frame, squeeze through sideways with a basket of dirty laundry, keep my balance without dropping said basket while repeatedly shifting the position of my foot to prevent a persistent ferret (often two or three ferrets by this time) from sneaking past me.

Sometimes the ferret(s) won, leaving me to hunt them down and coax them out from under the washing machine, water conditioner or freezer, or from behind any number of boxes, paint cans, or other dirty remnants of life. Pogo and Gizmo were easy; make with the squeaky toy, and they came running. Boys! But Widget refused to succumb to such mundane tactics, and she didn't often fall for the same trick more than once. The sound of a door opening to one of several forbidden-to-ferrets domains *might* get the better of her curiosity, and she'd emerge from her current hiding place in anticipation of exploring new turf. Sometimes a dab of Nutrical, a vitamin supplement that ferrets love, on the tip of my finger could lure her out, but this was a 50/50 proposition at best. She was clever enough to poke her head out just far enough to lick up the treat, but not far enough for me to grab her.

If there were such a thing as an exotic princess ferret, Widget, with her dark eyes and gorgeous coat, would fit the bill to a T. One case in point: All ferrets can open a door if it isn't pulled to, and Widget was no exception. Princess Widget, however, would wait by a closed door for one of the "boys," Pogo or her brother Gizmo to open it for her. And to see her turn her nose up as Pogo and Gizmo chased and fought over various squeaky toys in macho ferret fashion while she waited for "her" toy (a soft fuzzy ball with a bell inside) to be tossed to her...too funny.

And to think I almost lost her when she was only about thirteen weeks old! I noticed that she ingested—not just chewed—the bedding in the cage. Large holes appeared in different blankets and sheets. I thought she might lose this behavior if I moved her to an isolation cage with no blankets or sheets, but only carpet tiles on which to sleep. To my dismay, I noticed chewed corners of the carpet tiles while the food in her bowl remained untouched. This was no life for a ferret, and I made the agonizing decision to have her put to sleep. But my veterinarian saw the pain in my eyes and suggested some tests for Widget to see what was happening. Maybe she could be saved. An x-ray revealed a large mass in her stomach, probably all the bedding she'd swallowed. The biggest danger the mass presented was that it could cause a lethal blockage, so the vet prescribed tiny doses of a feline laxative that might break up the mass and allow it to pass through Widget's intestines. She also suggested I begin to feed Widget a special high-potency food to replace some of the nutrients she'd lost while dining on blankets. I saw little difference in Widget's behavior over the next day or two, but one day in the supermarket I saw a bag of cat food specifying hairball control. Hmm. I used to feed my ferrets cat food before being sold on the benefits of actual ferret food, and never had a problem. Maybe time to move away from designer food and return to what always worked in the past. When I put some of the new food in Widget's bowl, she gobbled it like a champ. Bon appétit, little girl! Gizmo and Pogo liked the new food as well. Widget gained weight, the mass must have dissolved, bedding no longer doubled as ferret chow, and Widget moved back in with her friends.

Goofy as he was, when it came to playtime with the squeaky, Pogo focused just like any of his wild kin that hunted prairie dogs. When I squeezed the squeaky, Pogo awoke in an instant, made the mandatory stop to his litter box, and was out of his cage like a shot to capture the toy and express deliver it to one of several hiding places, usually under the bed, under one of the nightstands, or in the "ferret condo" that Vinny had made for them.

But Gizmo made Pogo look like a rank amateur when it came to a squeaky match. Maybe the sound of the squeaky when I squeezed it mimicked that of a small animal and triggered some visceral instinct causing my sweet Gizmo to became unhinged when he heard it. More than once, he got so excited in his attempts to capture it that he couldn't even see the squeaky and jumped in a blind frenzy toward the general area of the sound, catching my hand, finger, or leg instead, often drawing blood. Gizmo didn't have a mean bone in his body, but he became the ferret equivalent of Stevenson's Mr. Hyde when his predatory instincts held sway. I learned the hard way to always wave the squeaky in front of him to recapture his focus, and always, always protect my flanks. The safest way to play with Gizmo was to throw the squeaky and let him chase it so he, like Pogo, could retrieve it, run away with it, and stash it somewhere. A more dangerous version of the game allowed him to have one end of the toy while I held the other and continued to make it squeak. Gizmo's hisses while his eyes glazed over as he entered a near-hypnotic trance while fighting for possession of the toy sometimes creeped me out. The good thing about this game was that so long as Gizmo's teeth were sunk in the squeaky, they weren't imbedded in my flesh.

It's important to note here that before we released the ferrets from their cage to the wide world of "house," Vinny and I followed a strict ferret-proofing checklist that included shutting all necessary doors and drawers, removing certain objects off the floor, and uncovering their remote litter box (on the off-chance one of them might use it instead of the nearest corner). But there were times when even the most elaborate precautions proved inadequate. One evening in particular, Vinny and I made the cardinal mistake of forgetting the ferrets were on the loose. When we came to our senses and set out to round them up, Pogo and Gizmo were corralled within minutes. Widget was nowhere to be found. Door to garage closed? Check. Laundry room door closed? Check. Dishwasher door closed? Check. Bedroom doors closed? Bathroom closet door closed? Check. Doors under the kitchen sink and bathroom sink closed? Check. Right down the list. Nothing left undone. Into what new devilry had she gotten herself this time? Within half an hour, which felt more like an eternity, I was a wreck. Panic had its way with me as I envisioned Widget trapped in some hole in the wall or, worse, outside the house having fallen prey to a hungry hawk.

Vinny attempted to reassure me that wherever Widget was, she'd show up when she was ready. "This is just typical Widget," he said. As I sat in the living room wringing my hands and waiting for Vinny to bring me a promised glass of wine, I heard him laugh from the kitchen, and then a triumphant, "Found her!" I ran into the kitchen, and to my unbridled delight and amazement, I saw Widget looking quite comfortable and none the worse for wear reclining inside the refrigerator on the bottom ledge between the door and the salad crisper drawers. I couldn't believe it. She must have jumped in at some point while we had the door open, and we didn't see her because of her light coloring. Little Silver Streak.

The major downside of keeping ferrets as pets is that they're not with us very long. The large majority of them develop some form of cancer, and depending upon the degree to which their quality of life diminishes and how much they appear to be suffering, a trip to the vet to end their misery usually occurs between five and seven years. After Pogo and Widget were put down, I realized I'd had enough heartbreak and decided to buy no more ferret babies, but I didn't want Gizmo to be lonely. A friend told me of a local ferret rescue center where I might find an adult cage mate for my Giz. Seemed like a good idea. Give an unwanted or abandoned ferret a second chance at a good life, especially when the man who ran the shelter assured me that all animals up for adoption had been vet checked and found to be in good health.

Vinny again chose to remain home while I went to select my ferret, and again, I returned with two. Bella and Cricket had arrived at the shelter together and had bonded. So, of course, I took them both. When the two girls were introduced to Gizmo, a short wrestling match ensued among the three to establish dominance before they became friends, curled up together, and went to sleep.

A 20-foot length of aluminum duct tubing provides a clear demonstration of how one ferret's intelligence level differs from that of another. When Gizmo was younger, he figured out by himself in short order that if I held the squeaky inside one end of the tubing, all he had to do to get at it was enter the tunnel from the other end. It didn't matter how I twisted and turned the tubing or how far away I placed one end from the other, Gizmo followed the tubing around and then flew through the tunnel to grab the squeaky. Cricket, even with "lessons," didn't get it for a long time. Regardless of how close I placed one end of the tunnel to the other, she persisted in digging and scratching at the location where I held the squeaky inside the tube unless I placed her head inside the other end of the tube. After much special "tutoring," she began to get the hang of it.

The now five-year old Gizmo had begun to slow down, and milky cataracts partially covered his eyes. But Bella, whom I'd had for less than a year, declined much faster. A hefty ferret when I brought her home, she began dropping weight at an alarming rate. The vet confirmed she had a mass in her stomach which might be treated with Prednisone. I'd had a bad experience in the past with Pogo and that drug, so I opted just to keep an eye on Bella. While she continued to lose weight, she still played with Cricket and Gizmo for short periods of time, and I hesitated to have her put to sleep. But then one day after many days of her feeling like she had no body mass at all when I picked her up, I noticed that even though she went to the food bowl, she wasn't eating. She was, in truth, starving. I had no choice but to make the difficult and only humane decision.

Within a couple of months of losing Bella, cataracts blinded Gizmo altogether although he still responded to the squeaky as best he could. He'd hear it but could only move his head from side to side while trying to get a bead on that which he couldn't see or locate unless I placed it in front of his nose. No longer did he grasp it with ferocity and attempt to pull it away from me, but rather, he'd just put his teeth on it and take a feeble step away with it. I'd give it to him without forcing him to struggle and then guide him to his favorite hiding place under the bookshelf. He couldn't find it by himself unless placed within a few inches of it. Such a difference from the bundle of energy he once was, and I wished for what seemed like the millionth time that an animal could speak to me and tell me if it was feeling sick or just old and tired.

Cricket is still going strong and, in fact, has gained considerable weight since I rescued her. No other ferret that I've owned has followed us around puppy style as much as Cricket. No matter where we go or how fast, Cricket is right there and has been stepped on or tripped over a couple of times as a result. She has no interest in the squeaky unless one of the "guys" had it, but she delights in chasing around a crocheted egg-shaped rattle. Unlike Gizmo and Pogo who attacked their squeaky with a vengeance, Cricket trots after the rattle and engages in tug 'o' war with me for short intervals before dropping it and wandering away feigning disinterest, only to return moments later for another try. When I give her possession of the rattle, she ambles over to her preferred hiding place inside the aluminum tubing. It's all very low key and nonferret-like, and I often wonder what kind of life she experienced before coming to live with us. I also wonder how she and Bella, two of the sweetest ferrets, wound up in a rescue facility. But better a shelter than abandoned on the street as so many animals are these days.

Twenty-two

I love sitting for Bear, an older Shepherd/Collie mix, who lives in the wilds of Schooley's Mountain with an untamed stand of woods behind the house. All sorts of creatures inhabit those woods, including fox and bears. I have seen neither of these denizens to date, but I've seen several deer, one which approaches to within four feet of the house at dinnertime and waits until I (or someone else) sit on the steps and throw bread or saltines to her. Bear is not happy with this arrangement and cannot reconcile himself to the temporary transfer of attention from him to a trespassing deer. I, however, think it's pretty cool to serve a deer one on one, but I wait with growing impatience to see a black bear. And I think this particular house on Schooley's Mountain offers the best chance to see one.

Robyn, one of Bear's owners, told me before my first gig with Bear that he was a nervous dog, and that even she was careful around him. She warned me against making any sudden movements or loud noises when near him. I noticed while sitting in the kitchen taking all this down that Bear assumed a protective posture around Robyn while he watched me with wary eyes.

Heeding Robyn's words and remembering Bear's timidity toward me, I walked into the house the first day of my initial assignment with him outfitted in heavy leather mid-forearm-length gloves, the kind one wears to reach into a lit fireplace to adjust a log. Bear barked something fierce when I entered the house, and then ran upstairs from where he watched me in ominous silence. Under Bear's supervision from on high, I unloaded my car. I put all my perishables in the fridge, read a note that was left for me by Robyn, and stacked my personal bags at the foot of the stairs. To avoid putting Bear on the defensive by carrying my luggage up to the landing where he stood guard, I had to bring him down to me. So, I grabbed his leash and uttered that most excellent of incantations, "Wanna go for a walk?" I learned right then as he hurtled down the stairs that Bear's bark is far worse than his bite. In a word, he's a mush, and I can't hug him or scratch him enough to his satisfaction.

Bear

Bear has a bit of arthritis in his hips for which he is given Dasuquin once a day, but he shadows me everywhere—upstairs, downstairs and, one time, into the shower. I have a small hiatal hernia that causes me to clear my throat pretty often. But Bear gets upset when I cough, even when I attempt to suppress it by covering my mouth with my hand. If sleeping, he wakes up and looks at me with a concerned expression on his face, snuggles closer, or sometimes barks and runs to the window. One morning while in the shower, I coughed and then saw his head and front paws appear inside the shower curtain. And I watched in amazement and some horror as this full-grown dog with arthritic hips scrambled all the way into the tub with me and remained there tolerating the hot water raining on his head and back. I mentioned this incident to Robyn later who said he'd been known to do that during thunderstorms, but she couldn't remember him doing it on other occasions.

Bear protects his home from anything or anyone that he suspects doesn't belong in the picture. He barks at the UPS truck that passes by the house on the street. He barks at the intrepid deer that trespass on his lawn in search of a snack. He barks at phantoms that he alone can see, sometimes in the middle of the night. Nothing like being in a deep sleep and jolted awake by the bark of a large dog sleeping on the floor beside your bed.

Rob and Robyn subscribe to the philosophy of letting all living creatures be as I found no insecticide anywhere in the house one night when in dire need of such a weapon. I was watching *Columbo* with Bear when some movement on the carpet pulled my focus. A cave cricket! *Yikes!* I pulled my feet up onto the sofa and watched the cricket amble across the living room. Such arrogance for a bug! When it disappeared under one of the armchairs, Bear curled up beside the chair, and I had no trouble believing that he, too, had seen the blasted insect and was crushing it with his body while protecting me—much as a child believes her daddy protects her by vanquishing all monsters from under the bed. Unlike the aforementioned child who would harbor some doubts about Dad's anti-monster prowess if she continued to hear menacing growls in the bedroom, I continued to believe that Bear had made the cricket be no more even after he moved from the chair leaving no trace of an ex-creature on the carpet. *Alas!* The reappearance of the cricket shattered my fantasy once and for all of Bear coming to my rescue comic-book-hero style. The cricket continued to disappear and reappear over the course of the evening. By happy chance, it never had the temerity to venture between the coffee table and sofa where I perched, although it did once eye the far end of the sofa. I leaned way over the edge with my legs crossed Indian style so I could see where the cricket went and exhaled with relief when it changed course at the last second and headed away from the sofa and me toward another armchair. I hoped as I'd never hoped before that the cricket couldn't or wouldn't climb or jump onto the furniture so that next time I saw it, it would be on the back of the sofa inches from my face.

Felt like forever passed before I found the nerve to jump off the sofa and sprint out of the living room to the kitchen where I rooted around for a large clear bowl which I could drop over the cricket when next I saw it. Found a loaf pan that looked like a good candidate for cricket containment, and after making sure it lay flush against the carpet when upside down (taking no chances that an encapsulated cricket could stage a breakout), I returned to the living room and waited. As fate would have it, my creepy adversary made no further appearance, and as the *Columbo* credits rolled, I realized I'd devoted the last hour and a half to studying the ways and means of a cave cricket.

Further evidence of Rob's and Robyn's reluctance to kill or interfere with wildlife came in the form of an enormous hornets' nest attached to the outside of their eleven-year-old daughter's bedroom window. I had not been forewarned about the nest and first saw it when I pulled my car into the garage and happened to look up. I had never seen a nest so large. It was massive. Measuring over a foot in length, at least eight inches wide, not counting an arm that extended two-thirds of the way across the entire window, it was a frightening thing to see. Judging by the number of hornets and their level of activity, I thought they had it in mind to build the Trump Tower of nests. Brooke, the daughter who shares her window with the hornets, is fascinated by the nest and has watched it grow from its earliest stages. I checked out the nest from inside the bedroom and admit to feeling queasy at the sight of all those hornets separated from me by only a pane of glass. Amazing and terrible at the same time. While scary to behold, I had to admire the incredible feat of architectural engineering achieved by the hornets.

Rob and Robyn have no intention of removing or destroying the nest. They consider it, in Robyn's words, "one of God's science projects," and an educational opportunity for their three young children who get to see the inner workings of a hornet nest up close and personal.

The last time I visited with Bear and an adopted three-month old kitten, Willow, only an abandoned nest remained. But it continued to disturb me, despite it having lost the power to draw me to it several times a day out of morbid curiosity.

Twenty-three

Duncan, a Welsh Corgi, was less than a year old when I first met him. He was and is very smart, very charismatic, and very energetic, the kind of dog with whom I love spending time. Not only is Duncan a fun-loving dynamo who challenges me to keep up with him, but my living quarters while with him are pretty swank. I have a charming private apartment, complete with laundry and full kitchen that's no more than 100 feet from the water of a Lake Hopatcong cove. Sliding glass doors open onto the patio from where I cross a small bit of lawn and walk out onto the dock, sometimes accompanied by Duncan sporting his life jacket in case he can't contain himself if he sees a duck swimming by that looks just a little too uppity. For creature comforts, I have a grill, fire pit, kayaks, and a hot tub at my disposal. Pet sitting does have its perks!

Nancie, Duncan's owner, provides me with the key to the front door of the main house above the apartment if the walkway and steps leading down to the apartment are impassable because of snow. Early one such winter morning when snow obscured the path to the apartment, although the driveway and front steps had been cleared, I needed to head out to do some run-of-the-mill but necessary errands. Missions accomplished, I returned to the house but couldn't open the front door because I'd forgotten to set the toggle buttons to the "open" position before I'd engaged the deadbolt. (Didn't know at the time that, with the toggle buttons in "closed" position, all I needed to do was turn the key a little harder to unlock the door.) But I had the apartment key with me and began to scoop out (with my hands) the snow-covered side walkway. It didn't look like too terrible a job at first blush, but my gloves were not of the super warm or waterproof variety since I hadn't planned on having to immerse them in snow. Two or three scoops convinced me that there had to be an easier way to make my way down to the apartment door. Well, Duncan had walked on top of the snow crust for the last day or so. "But you weigh more than Duncan," whispered the voice of reason in my head. "And you have a compromised aching knee." Ignoring said voice (almost never a wise decision), I abandoned my scooping endeavors in favor of sitting down and pushing off down the snowy slope that obscured the pathway steps. I reached the bottom by the apartment entrance, stood up, dusted the seat of my pants, and walked/glided across the snow to the door only twice sinking to midcalf in the white stuff. Duncan looked at me from his crate as if I were nuts when I unlocked the glass doors, possibly because I had chosen this day to frolic in the snow wearing sneakers instead of boots.

Duncan

Later that same morning, I again headed out the front door, this time with Duncan for his mid-morning recess on the front lawn, and this time garbed in a pair of warm snow boots. I reminded myself to adjust the toggle buttons, since I had made the conscious decision to leave the key inside rather than risk losing it in the snow.

A raw, cloudy day in which Mother Nature suffered from sneezing fits of freezing rain. And a day on which the universe decided to have one of its frequent laughs on Stormie.

No sooner had Duncan gotten his nose into the wind than he catapulted down the front steps jerking me with him before my other hand had released the door knob, and before I'd changed the toggle buttons. *Slam!* The instant I heard that sound, the finality of the door closing and locking, a stifling sense of utter helplessness almost overwhelmed me. Nancie was scheduled to return the next day, and I'd planned to dedicate this day to restoring the apartment to the state it was in when I'd arrived. Instead, all I could think about was the time that would be wasted while I figured out how to get back into the house. The keys to the front and back doors—locked inside. The keys to my car—locked inside. My cell phone—locked inside. My file with Nancie's cell phone number—locked inside. Nothing for it but to look for somebody who might loan me a phone. After knocking in vain at three houses (I forgot to mention that this particular escapade happened on a Friday when most everyone was at work.), I found another human outside (a dog-owned human) who loaned me his phone so I could call Vinny for a ride home (with Duncan), so I could get on the computer where I store copies of all my files, so I could look up Nancie's cell number and call her in Florida, so she could give me instructions on how to get into the house. A lot of dots to connect, but they did all connect. Thank you, universe.

Two hours after I made the ill-fated decision to leave the house without a key in my possession, I regained access to the house with a spare key that Nancie had given to a neighbor for just such emergencies. I picked up where I'd left off putting the apartment back together while Duncan stretched out in front of the fireplace, maybe dreaming about the ferrets he smelled when at my house but never got to meet.

The following autumn, I returned to Duncan who had learned the word "squirrel" and went berserk whenever he heard the word or saw one in the flesh. As soon as we were outside, he looked for them with obvious malice aforethought, stopping at different points in the driveway and staring fixedly at certain trees where he knew squirrels hung out. Nancie suggested I always keep Duncan on a leash, even if we didn't go beyond the front lawn. In Duncan's mind, giving chase to a squirrel always trumped a human's existence as the authority figure. When returning from a walk, Duncan would again scope out the front yard before heading down the path to the apartment where he knew he always received a treat. Treats rank high in Duncan's hierarchy of must-haves. So, I'd release him at the top of the walkway leading to the apartment and let him run down by himself to wait for me at the door. This practice worked well until the morning he morphed into a little devil. As he took off down the side of the house, he grabbed a Frisbee from the ground and disappeared behind the hot tub with it. No big deal. I turned to unlock the door and then called him. Nothing! I walked around the hot tub. Not there. I ran to the edge of the water. Not there either. A glance up the path and into the neighbors' yard also revealed no trace of Duncan. I looked up at the deck. No Duncan. With images of him lying injured in the street, I half-walked, half-ran around the other side of the house where I saw the Frisbee lying on the ground. I continued my jog to the front of the house. And then I saw him—on the far side of the neighbors' front lawn near the edge of the street! A good 200 feet away! When he heard me call him and saw me, he sat down where he was and looked at me almost inviting me to come after him and play. I didn't dare chase him but instead called him to me. As luck would have it, he ran to me but continued past me down to the back of the house. I am certain he knew he was being bad because it took another three or four minutes to get him inside while he ran tight circles around me. All I can figure is he saw one of those confounded squirrels and took off after it. And when he realized he could outrun me, well, a new game began. Duncan had a blast; Stormie not so much. From that point on, Duncan lost all his off-leash privileges with me.

I told Nancie what had happened, and she confirmed what I had just learned, "No one has fun when Duncan is off-leash except Duncan."

But there is one exception, one distraction which appears to override all else, including Frisbees, other people, ducks, and possibly deer and squirrels. Bubbles! Duncan loves bubbles and will chase them *ad infinitum*, breaking them with his mouth. A bubble gun which emits several bubbles at a time sends Duncan into fits of delirium as he dashes around, leaps and barks while trying to pop each one, including those that come to rest on the ground. I had a scary moment when one bubble gun trigger broke while in the middle of an all-out game of bubble popping. Duncan watched me with growing impatience as I tried to get it to work. He followed me inside and performed every trick he knew as I attempted to repair it. For all his intelligence, he didn't understand that I couldn't play with him, much as I wanted to. I ordered a second bubble gun online. And while rummaging around in the bag of Duncan paraphernalia that Nancie had left me, I located an old-fashioned bubble maker, the kind in which you dip a wand into a solution and then blow one or two bubbles at a time. It tided him over for the couple of days it took for the new bubble gun to arrive. When I opened the package, Duncan recognized the bubble gun at once for what it was and made it clear that he wanted to play. He was ecstatic, and so was I. It's the only bit of entertainment I've found so far that can wear him out. A tired Duncan is a quiet Duncan.

I have since managed to break every bubble gun, three in all, with which I've played with Duncan, and Nancie wonders if I release all my suppressed anxiety into the luckless triggers. If only I could rig and operate a cast iron bubble gun!

Twenty-four

L ife's craziness. It sucks us into a maelstrom of agitation and drives us to race from one task to another to another before we finish even one. And depending upon the quality of sleep we had the previous night or the promptness with which we get our early morning caffeine fix, be it coffee, tea, soda or chocolate, or the uncooperative weather, or any number of other variables, we can early on become sitting ducks before the day's onrush of demands. At day's end, we survey with bewilderment all the tasks in various stages of "undoneness" and wonder how we accomplished so little when we never stopped moving for five minutes. An all-too-common scenario, especially for those of us who approach vintage years. Now kick into the mix of adrenalin-raising impositions the preparation for family vacation, that event almost guaranteed to push chaos and stress levels into the realm of insanity. Some time ago, I had the opportunity to witness the "fallout" from what I can only term the *Home Alone* syndrome (based on the movies of the same name).

While I was not present for the morning hubbub at my clients' home before they left for vacation, I can imagine the scene: Susan preparing breakfast for David and Matthew. Susan or David feeding and walking Jada. The checking and rechecking of lists to ensure everything was packed that needed to be packed. The loading of the car. All happening while Matthew, like any young boy, bounced around with excitement, getting underfoot, and causing yet more distraction.

All systems "go." Everyone and everything in the car. Sighs of relief as breathing rates slowed to normal. And then, an hour or so later, *JADA!* Susan called me in a panic: "We're on the road heading for our hiatus from real life! Would you be able to care for Jada while we're away?"

Yeah, life is crazy. It's a wonder we ever get any of our chips to fall the right way. But we can be thankful that we're not the ones with whom ultimate control rests.

Twenty-five

One of the most difficult dogs left in my care was Dior, a young unmanageable miniature poodle.

During my meet-and-greet interview, Nina, Dior's owner, told me she was at her wit's end as to what to do with the anxious, insecure—but, deep down, really sweet—Dior. He barked nonstop, pooped in the house, hated other dogs, snapped at people without warning and, in general, comprised a pint-sized major headache. Would I, knowing Dior's idiosyncrasies, be willing to sit with him for a week while the family went away? I had some reservations, but because I was still building my clientele pool, I committed to the assignment.

As with so many owners of problem dogs, Nina's MO of dealing with Dior's barking was to give him treats to keep him quiet, treats after walking, treats just because. Lots of dog owners don't get that dogs interpret rewards in reinforcement terms, not preventative terms. When dogs are offered treats in response to barking, for instance, they think along the lines of, "Okay, if I bark, I get a treat." Hence, barking behavior remains unchecked, sometimes worsens, and all too often results in the dog being taken to a shelter, left on the road abandoned, or taken to a veterinarian to be put down.

I walked into the empty house the first day of my assignment feeling more than a little apprehensive and armed only with a fair amount of knowledge gleaned from other animal handlers and from my own experience. Dior met me at the door with nonstop hysterical barking until I rattled his leash. Like most dogs when anticipating a walk, he calmed down within seconds and appeared happy and eager for company.

I was surprised by how well Dior walked on a leash when he was the only dog on the street. But the sight of another dog triggered a ballistic response from Dior, complete with frantic aggressive barking and deranged leaping at the end of his leash in an attempt to get at the other dog that, in most cases, was larger than he. In short, so long as Dior succumbed to the stimulus of another dog, I ceased to exist in his mind, a dangerous-for-all situation. In response to Dior's frenzy and regardless of what it took on my part (smacking him on the rump, pushing him down multiple times until he stayed, shortening his leash to a few inches in length), I always forced him to sit until he once again focused on me. Sometimes I wonder how a random cell phone camera might capture my training of Dior as I demanded that he sit still, even after the offending dog had moved on. In short, the first several walks with him were a struggle, a battle of wills, between Dior and me. But one invaluable nugget I had learned as a dog handler was that in any competition with a dog, I had to win at all costs. By the end of the week, Dior was much better behaved, calmer, and happier. While he still sailed into Rambo Land and forgot about me at the sight of another dog, he returned to reality and to me with much less effort on my part than he had a few days earlier. I had high hopes for the little guy.

Nina had also told me that Dior refused to sit for his meals. It seems he would not set his butt on the cold tiled floor in the laundry room where his bowls were located. Seriously? Well, if he wanted to eat while in my care, he would lose that demigod attitude in a hurry. Sure enough, by end of week after my relentless and consistent verbal and physical cues that he sit on the uncarpeted floor before I placed his food dish down for him, he got the idea and obeyed without hesitation.

I refused to offer him treats in response to his incessant barking in the house. Rather, I just firmly commanded him to "Stop!" and walked away. In this area, too, he showed much improvement by week's end unless I was in the shower when he realized he could bark to his heart's content, and there was nothing I could do about it. I never said he was a stupid dog!

Dior was, at heart, a snuggle bug. He loved nothing better than curling up close to me on the sofa for hours while I watched television or read a book. However, I learned to always keep an eye on him. Whenever he left the living room and headed for the dining room (his favorite place to poop in the house), I grabbed him and took him outside. Most times, he rewarded my diligence by then doing his business where he should. In these instances alone, I rewarded him with a treat. By the end of the week, he would sometimes jump off the sofa, look at me, and go to the door to be let out. Good boy!

Dior loved bedtime. At night when I turned off the downstairs lights, he raced up the stairs and waited in the bedroom for me to lift him onto the bed. He looked forward to snuggling under the covers at my feet or on the other pillow next to my head. A cozy time. But cozy time almost always was negated in the morning by my having to leap out of bed, grab my slippers and bathrobe, and get him outside before he jumped off the bed and pooped on the upstairs hall carpet. No early morning luxurious stretches for me. And with only a week in which to work, I could come up with no feasible solution for this problem.

At week's end, I wrote a long, detailed note recapping my week with Dior and describing my methods and his improvement in detail. I admonished Nina, her husband and daughter to follow my practices to avoid any backsliding on Dior's part. The dog showed a lot of promise for developing into a wonderful family pet.

Several months later, Nina called upon me again for pet care. In response to my question about Dior's behavior, she said, "Terrible, just terrible." Her husband hated the dog, and neither she nor her daughter had time to devote to Dior's training. A discouraging scenario indeed.

Feeling frustrated, I returned to Dior, restarted from square one, and again realized steady improvement in his behavior over the few days I had with him. I left another letter for Nina advising that every effort be made to continue what I had started. Dior was a smart, teachable dog and like all dogs, was happier when he had boundaries and knew his place in the hierarchy of his human family.

Weeks passed, and I heard nothing from Nina as to Dior's progress. On a whim, I decided to reach out to Nina and felt saddened to hear her sing the same old lyrics. She loved Dior but just didn't have time for him and wished she could find a good home for him. During our conversation, I recommended a well-known, highly successful (but expensive) professional animal trainer to her. She called Ben and was delighted with the results he got from Dior.

JOYCE AND DIOR

The next time Nina called, I had committed to another client for the dates she needed me, but I recommended a friend who had helped me out in the past with animal care. I told her Joyce was a reliable gentle person who loved dogs but had less experience with animals than I. Nina agreed to meet Joyce, and the three of us scheduled a meet and greet shortly after Dior's last session with Ben. I was delighted by the change in Dior. He barked for only a minute or two when we rang the bell, and he appeared more secure and much calmer than I'd ever seen him. Nina said Dior was now trained to always sit while his food dish was put down, and to poop on newspaper in the laundry room rather than the dining room carpet if he needed to go out when no one was around. I felt comfortable leaving Joyce alone with Dior for two weeks, a longer gig than I had ever had with him.

I gave Joyce a copy of my file on Dior and advised her that if Dior barked and did not seem receptive to her when she arrived, she should just rattle his leash. Dior would come running.

But things went wrong from the get-go, and Joyce did not have an easy time of it. Dior, since our meet and greet, and unbeknown to me, had been put on Prozac. Far from responding well to Joyce when she rattled his leash, he bit her when she attempted to attach the leash to his collar. Maybe he sensed some fear in Joyce. Maybe the Prozac exacerbated his latent aggressive tendencies. But from that point on, Joyce wore protective oven mitts whenever she approached the dog. I remained in frequent contact with Joyce over the next two weeks and according to Joyce, Dior never warmed up to her even when it was time to go for a walk. To the contrary, he snapped at her several times. Of course, Joyce didn't feel comfortable picking him up, let alone allowing him to sleep on the bed with her. So, Dior slept in his crate. All in all, a terrible two weeks for Joyce, and I have always regretted enrolling her in that assignment. I give her enormous credit for sticking it out and not demanding that I make other arrangements mid-way through the assignment.

Nina confessed later that, even though she'd laid out a small fortune for Ben, she had discontinued his training regimen for Dior, opting instead for the Prozac regimen, before Joyce arrived.

LAST TIME WITH DIOR

The following year, Nina called and asked if I could care for Dior for a few days, beginning the next day. She had an out-of-state funeral to attend. Given the circumstances, I agreed despite having decided that I was done with the dog.

Nina told me that Dior was still taking Prozac, which at least in theory helped calm him.

When I arrived at the house, I was horrified by the change I saw in Dior. He uttered no sound, but cringed inside his crate (although the door was open) with his nose on his paws, and glared at me in distrust out of the top of his head. I knew not to approach him while he assumed that timid defensive posture. Had Dior exhibited the same body language when Joyce had been there the previous year? If so, Joyce, having received no prior warning from me, might have failed to recognize and interpret the dog's fearful posture and thought this was normal Dior demeanor when a stranger first entered the house.

Dior camped in his crate maintaining the same posture and attitude for nearly two hours. And then a light bulb went on in my head! Ring the doorbell in hopes that Dior's natural tendency to alert the intruder of his presence would override whatever thought processes were circulating in his Prozac-riddled mind. Success! At the sound of the bell, he barked and dashed from his crate to the front door. Once he realized he'd been tricked, however, he skulked away from me, but he did not return to his crate. Instead, he lay down on his bed in the living room while keeping a steadfast wary eye on me. I sat on the sofa and became engrossed in Wimbledon. While I watched the match, Dior ventured further into the room and jumped onto a sofa other than the one on which I sat. Then he moved onto the same sofa as me and crept next to me. I pet him, stood up, and walked over to where his leash hung. It had to have been at least five or six hours since he'd last been outside before I arrived. Dior responded with enthusiasm to the leash rattle. And we were good.

But since the last time I had seen him, Dior had developed the nasty, what-can-only-be-described-as-spiteful habit of refusing to poop while walking. Instead, upon returning from walks, he would do his business on the dining room carpet (as opposed to the newspaper). This happened several times until once, after yet another nonproductive long walk and yet another deposit on the dining room carpet within five minutes of being home, I grabbed him and put his nose in his mess. He turned and snapped at me, catching the edge of my hand. Such behavior is unacceptable and unforgivable, so I grabbed him by the scruff with him twisting and squirming in an attempt to get another piece of me, and put him in his crate for the night.

By the next morning, Dior was fine and appeared happy to see me. I don't know if the previous night's incident had been his way of "testing" me, but there were no more such incidents during my stay.

I have not seen Dior since 2015, three years ago. We are called upon to be good stewards of the animals that come into our lives, and the sad story of Dior tracks a dog's absolute psychological deterioration that occurs from lack of discipline and attention. Because of Nina's and her family's inability to spend time with him, Dior never had a chance to become a happy, well-adjusted family dog. Maybe Nina has since found him another home where the owners have time to spend with him, to train him and to love him. I hope so.

Twenty-six

Milano and Mia, two hyper but sweet Pomeranians, comprise one of the easiest assignments in my portfolio. Besides the fact that a large fenced-in yard obviates the necessity of walking the dogs, their owners always go above and beyond in their attempts to make things as effortless and comfortable for me as possible.

Only one concrete, set-in-stone, no-room-for-error rule: Close the front door before sliding open the baby gate at the top of the two foyer stairs to prevent the dogs, who are always right there to greet me, from running out of the house. Stephen and Teri accept my neurotic dislike of their grandfather clock bonging every half hour and laugh at my habitual halting of its pendulum. As they've told me many times, "Our home is your home. You're family. Make yourself comfortable." And I believe them. There's something warm and genuine about these two people, and despite their not being members of my church from where most of my cronies hail, I consider them two of my closest and most trusted friends.

Teri is a love who feels compelled to leave scores of Post-it notes all around the house, and several 81/2 x 11 pages of instructions detailing care of the dogs and the lengths to which she and Stephen have gone to make my life with her two "nut cases" (in her words) as easy and as enjoyable as possible. It doesn't matter to Teri that I took copious notes during our initial meet and greet two years ago and everything she writes, with few exceptions, is included in my file on Mia and Milano. If it makes Teri feel more secure to paper her walls and countertops with notes before leaving her fur babies for a week, so be it. I can live with that. It always makes me smile as I read each note and then toss them into a recycle bag. It's part of Teri's charm, and I love her, idiosyncrasies and all. She's as crazy, spontaneous and ridiculous as I am at times.

Milano (left) and Mia (right)

Teri fills individual small plastic sandwich bags with pre-measured kibble for each meal for each dog, leaving me with the herculean task of opening two bags at mealtime and spilling one into each bowl. She also fills the fridge with enough food (cold cuts, fresh vegetables, juice) to feed an army with the invitation to help myself to anything I want. And just before my arrival, she buys special food just for me despite my objections. These "special" supplies can and often do include fabulous pieces of filet mignon, fresh fruit, and my favorite flavor yogurt. Really, what's not to love about this woman?

Before we became friends, when I was nothing more than a reliable pet sitter for Milano and Mia, I mentioned to Teri that Vinny and I had booked a trip to Turks and Caicos where I would finally be able to tick off the number one item on my bucket list: ride a horse on the beach. Yay! And yes, it would be an expensive proposition at $150 per hour, but I counted it well worth the money for such a long-awaited experience. Sometime before Vinny and I were set to leave for our vacation, Teri called and asked that I stop by their house for lunch to go over a few changes in Mia's and Milano's routine before she and Stephen left for Aruba soon after we returned from Turks. Okay. After an enjoyable and informative visit, Teri said she wanted to pay me in advance for my upcoming assignment with the dogs. Thank you! And as she handed me the envelope of cash, she added—and I remember her words as if she spoke them to me yesterday, "There's a little extra in there. I know how much you're looking forward to riding a horse by the water, and I wanted to pay for you to do that." When I expressed reluctance to accept such a gift, Teri refused to budge saying she would share in my joy knowing she had helped make it happen. My eyes welled up as I sought to grasp the magnitude of such generosity.

My ride from Caicos Corral was scheduled for the last full day Vinny and I were in Turks, and it was a dream-come-true adventure despite my seat in the saddle not being what it had been years before. It was a private ride with just my amazing guide Jessica and me. Freckles, my horse, was a Thoroughbred and had been featured in the current issue of *Sports Illustrated*. He was a phenomenal animal, but I'd never before ridden a Thoroughbred and was unprepared for the speed with which he took off at a canter, almost a gallop, before I'd even gathered him up. But I managed to keep my seat. Woohoo! We rode along a mostly deserted stretch of beach, and Jessica pointed to a gigantic house up on the bluff saying that Prince had lived there at one time. When we turned for home, we rode in the warm green Caribbean Ocean. The horses loved it; it cooled them. I loved it; it soothed me, and it launched me into a state of euphoric oblivion. In short, the ride was everything I hoped it would be. Thank you so much, Teri!

Twenty-seven

This most difficult passage for me to write involves an area of my life that I wish I could deny and erase forever. Truth is no story of mine would be complete without including something of the dark underbelly of my character. Maybe we all cringe at some of the conscious decisions we've made in the past, but the things that gnaw at us with the most savagery involve those less-than-stellar character traits over which we feel we have no control.

I grew up in a family that put the "dys" in dysfunctional—an alcoholic father and a sadistic mother. And that's all I know. I know nothing about either of my parents' pasts or how they grew into the adults they did. With the exception of my paternal grandmother whom I loved with all my heart, but who died when I was fifteen, I don't even know my grandparents' names. My father was a mean drunk who posed no threat to me in a physical sense, but who took a good shot at devastating me psychologically and emotionally. Nina, his sister, reminisced on how Tom used to be such a "sweet little boy." Couldn't prove it by me. According to Nina, life happened, and all that sweetness turned into bitterness, bigotry, and rage. Cue the violins. I don't remember ever receiving one kind word from him or my mother, let alone enjoying any quality time spent with either of them.

What I do remember is being in junior high when a lot of the other kids somehow recognized my father's car when it was parked in front of Bunny's, one of the local gin mills. I bore constant bullying for several years about him being the town drunk. No thirteen- or fourteen-year old kid in the face of peer torment, thinks to say something like, "That's him. It's not me." And of course, I didn't even try to seek solace or support from my parents.

By the time I reached my mid-teens, I spent what little time I was home in my room upstairs attempting to escape the nonstop fighting between my parents and trying to avoid being dragged into the vicious name calling and general cruelty fostered by my father's drunkenness. When they could find nothing new to fight about, they fought old arguments over and over again. I could still hear the yelling through closed doors over my television or stereo, but I managed to shut most of it out.

Mealtimes were the worst, sitting mute at the table listening to my father rant on and on, night after night, about the stupid people with whom he worked or the nasty people who were in Bunny's where he always had "just one beer" on his way home. Or, when he was in rare form, he'd start in on my younger sister or my mother or me, finding fault with whatever his alcohol-marinated brain oozed. I began eating dinner in my room. It was better that way. I've been told by many who understand these things that one of the reasons I'm so thin is I associate food with unpleasantness.

Somehow, I suffered through my childhood, survived adolescence and my teen years, and sailed into young adulthood minus any support system or social guidelines. I had no blueprint to follow for a happy healthy lifestyle, not even a beginner's guide to appropriate adult behavior, and reached my early twenties clueless about what went into a mature, nurturing, grown-up relationship. Instead, I retained all the egocentric characteristics of a child. I was selfish, needy, tantrum-prone, love-starved, and far too ignorant to recognize genuine love from those who offered it to me. So, I destroyed several what-might-have-been satisfying and beautiful relationships by manipulating them into parent-child relationships, hurting myself and others in the bargain. And the more I failed at social skills, the more I hated myself, my parents, and my life. Fertile ground for big-time depression. And I was angry, so very angry.

We never had pets in the house when I was growing up with the exception of the occasional hamster and Chessie the kitten for a short time. A good thing for all animals but a sad state of affairs for most children and households in general. Animals contribute a sense of stability and coziness to a home, and they provide a non-judgmental ear to a troubled owner and often a warm body to hold and love when we most need to feel held and loved without fear of rejection.

After I'd graduated high school and moved out of the house, my parents somehow obtained a young yellow Lab. I don't know the circumstances under which they acquired Kelly, but I would guess she was either given to them or brought home from a shelter. Kelly was a sweet animal and did not deserve the miserable life she endured at the hands of my parents. The concept that a dog, like any animal, requires love and attention could not have crossed their minds even once. Kelly remained tethered in a dark basement room at least nine hours a day while my parents worked, plus any additional time when they might both be out of the house. Or when they were eating. Or any other time they didn't want to be bothered with her. When my mother returned home from work, she retrieved Kelly from the basement and chained her in the backyard. To the best of my knowledge, Kelly was never walked, never played with, never cuddled, never loved. It would not have occurred to my parents to take the time to train her, assuming she even needed to be trained. It was easier to just tie her up, leave her some water, and forget about her. Kind of the way they felt about my sister and me.

Those times when both my parents were home and engaged in their standard evening pastime of watching television in the den, Kelly lay at my father's feet and was not allowed to move until he fell into his drunken stupor. It was a disgusting tableau that I still see in as much detail as I did fifty years ago. My mother surrounded herself and gorged herself with bags of junk food, which were kept padlocked in my parents' bedroom during the day so my sister and I couldn't have any. My father almost always had a cigarette dangling from his mouth or fingers, and said cigarette often fell between the cushions of the sofa when he'd fallen asleep. How our house never caught fire and burned to the ground remains a mystery to me. At least, Kelly wasn't tethered during these times. If I were on Facebook now, I would insert a very sad or a very angry emoji here.

Whenever Kelly committed some infraction, and I can't imagine what "infraction" could have meant, my father kicked her and beat her without mercy with whatever he had handy, be it a magazine, an ashtray, a poker from in front of the fireplace, or his fist. It was a terrible thing to see, and when I was at the house, I interceded on Kelly's behalf several times. Such treatment of an animal today would be a reportable offense and, at the very least, would result in the removal of Kelly from that environment.

Some years later, and to my profound horror, I discovered that my father's streak of madness lived within me, but to a less frightening extent, even though I didn't drink. More often than I like to admit, I took my rage out on some of my own pets. It was like I became a different person and, despite loving animals with all my heart, there were times I stepped outside of myself while the devil had his way with my soul. I developed a desperate fear of this "other me." And I wondered many times if insanity was built into my DNA. An unabated racking guilt from my actions drove me to near suicide…and then to counseling and voluntary admission into a psychiatric hospital where I was diagnosed with clinical depression (anger turned inward).

Years (and many dollars) later, I managed to identify and, in large part, conquer my inner demons that would steal any and all joy from me. And I learned that my anger which I'd needed to survive when I was younger had long ago outlived its usefulness.

Decades have come and gone. I look back over the years and see how God's grace has upheld and calmed me. I was way too far gone to have calmed myself! He has blessed me with supportive and loving friends who have been invaluable in distancing me from the sick volatile environment in which I was raised. But depression, like any other illness, requires constant vigilance and discipline to manage. It lurks within me, just under the surface of rational thought and behavior. While I no longer fear it, I remain always mindful of its insidious stink.

I have begged forgiveness from God, as well as from those animals I mistreated. And though I believe I've been forgiven, I also believe that someday I will be judged and held accountable for my actions. I don't know why I had to go through such fire to get to where I am now, but I trust in the sovereignty of God and His perfect plan for me.

Clients and non-clients alike have told me that I have an extraordinary way with animals. I've never been afraid of non-humans (some bugs notwithstanding), and I never learned to hate them. Instead, I enjoy the company of animals and feel a kinship with them; they, in turn, trust me. A mutual respect exists between the four-legged denizens of our earth and me. Perhaps it always existed, but these days my connection to them is pure, unadulterated and not undermined by root rage.

Twenty-eight

Milano and Mia, the high-on-life Pomeranians, lay at my feet while I curled up in front of the television after dinner. I savored a rare period of calm before the dogs again sensed something amiss outside in the dark and went off the deep end barking with maniacal glee. And as I watched Jessica Fletcher write another murder, I ran my tongue along the inside of my teeth and retrieved something that felt very long, thick, and slimy from somewhere in my mouth.

In the split-second it took for me to envision a worm, register my overwhelming disgust, and acknowledge my consummate fear of not knowing what it was, I made the conscious decision to swallow it. Swallowing it seemed somehow less scary than spitting it out and seeing whatever it was. The thing slid down my throat with disturbing ease. *Gag!*

I spent the next several minutes attempting to justify my swallowing an unidentified gob of goo. It couldn't possibly have been some foreign matter because I surely would've felt something that large enter my mouth. An intense bitter taste interrupted my rationalizing, and my tongue felt kind of tingly numb like that feeling you get when you burn your mouth after trying to eat a forkful of baked potato that hasn't cooled enough yet.

The presence of this new symptom etched a bad scenario in my prone-to-hypochondria mind, which could convince me in no time flat that I had every disease listed in a PDR. Over the next hour or so my symptoms developed no further, and I resumed my "I'm okay" self-talk until I fell sleep having assured myself that if my tongue were to swell overnight, I would wake up and call 911.

When I awoke the next morning, I discovered with great relief that my mouth and all its inhabitants were back to normal, and I had neither grown another head nor lost the one I had. I still couldn't figure what had been in my mouth to make it feel so funky or to cause those symptoms...until I took my morning vitamins. And then it hit me. I take a large calcium capsule and a fish oil capsule with dinner. Because I swallow several supplements at once, vitamins occasionally lodge in the back of my mouth only to work themselves free later in the day. I think, this time, my tongue dislodged a large, not-quite-dissolved calcium capsule or fish oil capsule during its sweep of my mouth.

I wonder at the wisdom and depth of my fear, a fear that would have me swallow an unknown object rather than spit it out so I could identify it. And I know with remarkable clarity that if a similar situation were to occur, I would again swallow an unrecognized substance and consider the sanity of my action afterward.

Twenty-nine

Sometimes, I think that the grand truth of my life is stranger than fiction. Things—beautiful things, scary things, comedic things, odd and unexplainable things—find their way into my life more often than into the lives of most other people. At least, it feels that way to me sometimes. Maybe because I'm a double Pisces, metaphysical forces act upon me in greater quanta and with more regularity than on others often resulting in injury, especially to my feet. Whatever. I've given up trying to reason it all out and just accept that I attract far-out vibes from the universe, many of which supply me with a wealth of material from which to write my stories.

As I was growing up, I sustained more than my share of injuries. I've broken most of my toes and smashed my fingers at least once, which could have something to do with my being a Pisces who are prone to foot injuries according to astrological lore. Few activities were safe for me. A sled runner gauged the fingers of my right hand. I crashed my Harley years later and crushed the fingers of my left hand, my dominant hand, between a utility pole and the handlebars of the bike. My horse stepped on my foot, once that I remember. I showed up at work so often with one banged up body part or another that, after seeing me arrive at the office with yet another bandage, brace, or bruise, my manager at Bell Labs suggested that I take a gun to my head. It would be quicker, cheaper, and would save me a lot of grief. Halloween night 2009, I fell down an entire flight of stairs at a friend's house thinking I was going into the bathroom, and broke my entire maxillary process and orbital ridge, and badly sprained my ankle, wrist, and hand. The list goes on. You get the picture.

In addition, I've detailed some episodes earlier in this book proving beyond a reasonable doubt that I am a blueblood klutz. A good-hearted, dependable, somewhat intelligent, animal-loving klutz, but a klutz nonetheless. The force field through which I travel teems with mines just waiting for me to step on them and go *Boom!* Evidence of this phenomenon abounds throughout my stories.

And then there are the *really* strange events, those over which I have no control and can best be defined as sucker punches from an unknown dimension. Those that leave me scratching my head in bewilderment or laughing with incredulity, those incidents which defy rational thinking and which are too bizarre to be made up.

One morning when caring for Toby and Otis (my favorite Yorkie and Shih Tzu, respectively), I washed out my cereal bowl and pressed the button on the faucet hose attachment to change from stream to spray. The entire fixture came off in my hand! A horizontal jet of hot water shot across the kitchen soaking the floor and me. Little Otis, who had been lying on the floor behind me, bolted after being pelted by water droplets and surveyed the scene in disbelief from the safety of the hallway. The irony of the mishap lies in the fact that I hate washing dishes by hand and would, on any other given day, have put the bowl in the dishwasher. But, I figured, I'm here for only one more day. What can it hurt?

Thirty

HELLO, SASSY

Sassy, an eleven-year old Shih Tzu with more personalities jammed inside of her than one would think possible for such a small creature, was well-loved by her owner but had next to zero contact with people or other animals. Result: Sassy was a difficult dog to get to know.

My introduction to most dogs involves some cautious respectful gestures such as my getting down as far as necessary to the dog's level, holding my hand out, and speaking in soft, encouraging tones. A well-adjusted dog will respond by sniffing my hand, maybe licking it, and almost always welcoming a scritch behind its ears.

Sassy met me the first time with nonstop barking and her tail tucked well between her legs. She exhibited every sign of being the nervous dog she was by running up to me, always remaining just out of reach, and then away from me if I attempted to touch her. Ann, Sassy's owner, and the only person in whom Sassy held the slightest trust, quieted her for a few moments with a rawhide treat.

Raising her voice to be heard over Sassy's barking, Ann gave me the lowdown on Sassy care. And I, listening hard over the din, scribbled what Ann said on a piece of paper. First, Sassy was never to be walked; she was paper trained. But she did like to hang out on the enclosed deck in nice weather. Second, Sassy would bite anyone except Ann who attempted to pick her up. When Sassy was a puppy, a groomer had nicked her belly, an incident from which Sassy never recovered. Third, Sassy was a finicky eater and always had a bit of microwave-warmed chicken, hot dog, or meatball mixed in with her food. And fourth, Sassy would sleep on the bed with me. I love to have animals sleep next to me, but this little pup? I'd rather she didn't, at least until she had a chance to accept me.

The nerve-wracking meet and greet with Ann and Sassy behind me, I harbored serious doubts about whether I wanted to take on responsibility for this pint-sized neurotic. As a rule, I would rather deal with an aggressive dog than a timid dog. An aggressive dog is predictable; it will try to bite you. A timid dog might snap at any time without warning and, in my mind, makes a timid dog more dangerous than an aggressive dog. Had my only consideration been whether or not to follow my instincts, I'd have refused the assignment on the spot. But circumstances are almost never that simple, and they were not in this case. A trusted mutual friend had recommended me to Ann who was looking forward to reuniting with some high school friends she hadn't seen in years, and her previous pet sitter had canceled at the last minute. Better judgment yielded to conscience, and I accepted the five-day gig with Sassy.

I arrived at the house a week later to begin my assignment. Ann had already flown to Aruba for the reunion, but her daughter Dana met me at the door to make for an easier transition for Sassy. Didn't happen. Same old, same old with Sassy barking and running back and forth, even after being given a rawhide treat. Most dogs settle down when they hear me jingle their leash inviting them to go for a walk, but that option was off the table with Sassy. So, it became a matter of hoping she would wear herself out before I ran screaming from the house in frustration.

Things improved little after Dana left. While not afraid of Sassy, I felt uneasy being alone in that big house with Sassy racing up and down the hallway or, worse, hearing her bark from somewhere else in the house. I determined not to reward Sassy for barking or other bad behavior, but rather to ignore her until she made some kind of overture toward me.

To her credit, she ate most of her dinner and used the papers as she should. Small victories; I'll take 'em.

When it was time for bed, Sassy did not jump onto the bed with me but remained downstairs on a sofa in the living room from where she barked at frequent intervals throughout the night. This had to stop. How to get her into the bedroom if I couldn't pick her up and carry her? Around 2:30 in the morning, after being wakened for the umpteenth time by Sassy's barking, I remembered having seen a couple of baby gates in different rooms. If I could just corral her I thought in my semi-conscious state of mind, and herd her upstairs into the bedroom. Not so fast. As soon as Sassy saw me approaching with the gate, she jumped off the sofa and ran into another room. Then began a desperate game of catch me if you can between this canine terror and her half-crazed sitter with teeth clenched and eyes popping out of their sockets. Said game ended thirty minutes later after I'd barricaded all the downstairs rooms and herded her to the bottom of the stairs where she had no choice but to ascend them. I eventually scooched her into the bedroom, closed the bedroom door, and staggered into bed with every nerve in my body frayed to its limit. Sassy did not join me on the bed but allowed me four hours of uninterrupted sleep.

I'm forever grateful for neighbors who sleep soundly. Sassy's barking and yelping in protest to my corralling her in the wee otherwise silent hours of the morning raised the tiny hairs on the back of my neck. Anyone else who might have heard her theatrics could not have been blamed had they called the police in response to what sounded like clear animal abuse. Never again, I promised myself.

BRINGING DOWN THE HOUSE

Ann called upon me again later that year to care for Sassy while she vacationed in Lake Tahoe with the rest of her family. And because she had recently bought a new house, would I come by beforehand so she could show me around? Sure. So much for promises made to self.

The assignment began, and it became clear that Sassy did not remember me from five months earlier and carried on as she had when in her other house—incessant barking and running back and forth like a crazy thing. When she wore herself out barking, she adopted the more menacing behavior of stalking me in silence. This was a new trick. I'd walk down the hall of the long ranch-style house from one room to another, look behind me, and see Sassy several feet back staring at me. She'd stop when I stopped and "tiptoe" forward along the tiled floor when I began to walk again. Her stalking behavior continued throughout the day. A little unnerving to say the least.

When I first arrive on assignment at an unfamiliar house, I always take a few minutes to acclimate myself and put my charge(s) at ease before unpacking my bags. Sassy's antics shredded that agenda. After she had progressed to "stalking" mode, I emptied my suitcase and dropped the empty bag in a corner beside the bed. *Gasp!* I noticed with horror that the metal "foot" of my bag had slightly gouged the freshly painted wall of Ann's new house!

A frantic search of the garage yielded spackle as well as what looked to be matching paint. I called Vinny, who had proven throughout the years of living with me that he could fix or repair almost anything around the house that this reasonable facsimile of a bull in a china shop could break. He arrived the next day and spackled and repainted the wall so that it looked like new. But when dry, the fresh paint did not match exactly the three-month-old paint on the rest of wall even though it was the right color. We considered repainting the entire wall, but the bed's headboard was affixed to the wall. I'd never heard of doing such a thing, but there it was.

I felt sick while thoughts of self-condemnation filled my head. Only the second time Ann hires me, and I break her new house. Not to mention the fact that I am clueless about how to soothe her dog. What to do? Call her in California while she was on vacation? Out of the question! I decided instead to make the best of my remaining time at the house, focus on building a bridge to Sassy, and tell Ann about the bruised wall when she returned home.

My relationship with Sassy improved bit by tiny bit to the level of a tenuous mutual trust. A positive step, but any chance for peace I may have experienced in the beautiful wooded setting was negated by nagging feelings of embarrassment, self-disgust, and a desperate fear that Ann would sue an uninsured me, and I'd go to prison. And no one would ever hire me again. In short, my life as I knew it would be over.

I always leave a recap note for my client when I leave an assignment. My note to Ann ended with a request that she call me as soon as possible. I hated the ominous tone of it, but I felt that putting my "crimes" in writing rather than speaking with Ann in person was the way of a coward. Ann called me the day after she returned home, and I confessed to the dent in the wall and Vinny's and my unsuccessful efforts to repair it. I asked if we could unfasten the headboard and repaint the entire wall. Her instant response astounded me. "Don't worry about it," she said. "We raised three girls and sustained much more damage than a ding in the wall over the years. Didn't even notice it. Let it go. Don't give it a second thought." Ahh, sweet mercy! I was almost in tears with relief and gratefulness.

As an aside, I have been blessed with a pool of generous and forgiving clients who seem to take my penchant for butterfingers in stride. One client and friend, Sue, used to have me sit her two elderly cats, Flash and Gordon, when she and her husband were away. I loved those assignments—feed the kitties breakfast, a mid-morning nosh, and dinner. Clean their litter boxes. Done! And such a house! An antique-filled Victorian-style hideaway set back from the road and nestled in acres of beautiful woods. In a word, a retreat that never failed to refresh my soul and provide a place of quiet, peace, and long journeys into daydreams.

Sue, a culinary ace, maintained a well-stocked kitchen and always prepared some kind of meal ahead of time for me "just to get you started," she would say, and baked a jar full of cookies to satisfy my monster sweet tooth. So, there I was one afternoon, poking my nose into the fridge for a snack when Sue's ceramic butter dish crashed to the floor and shattered because I'd forgotten to close the little plastic door that prevents such accidents from happening. After cleaning up the mess, I went online to find an identical butter dish and order it for her. Success in finding one, but unsuccessful in having it delivered before she and her husband, Don, returned home. Yet again, my conclusion note contained an apology for doing damage and yet again, a client laughed it off and, in this case, even returned my money to me.

HELLO, HERO

Dana and her husband, Paul, owned an elderly Belgian Shepherd that they kenneled when the family went away. A couple of years after I'd begun sitting with Sassy, some changes happened in the kennel that made Dana uncomfortable, and she contacted me asking if I'd be willing to care for Hero and Sassy together at their house while she and her family went on vacation. Being partial to larger dogs and Shepherds in particular, I jumped at the opportunity to care for Hero.

And as an added incentive, in case I needed one, Dana assured me that Sassy got along well with Hero. He soothed her. Perfect!

The meet and greet with Hero went as well as my initial meeting with Sassy had gone badly. Hero was big, even for a Belgian Shepherd, with a head the size of a dinner plate—a true and handsome gentle bear. I loved him on sight and received a firsthand demonstration of how well-trained Hero was. Paul, Dana, and I walked Hero down the street. I held the leash as we walked until Paul told me to drop the leash. I did so, and Hero stopped until I retrieved the leash. At dinnertime, Paul filled Hero's bowl, put it down, and asked Hero to "sit" and "wait." Hero obeyed without argument and did not make a move toward his dish until Paul said, "Okay."

Hero exuded charm and personality, the likes of which I haven't seen often in another dog. When Hero became excited or wanted something—a treat, for instance—he would "dance." There's no other word for it. He rocked like a child's rocking horse. If he saw the mail truck outside or anything else that he thought didn't belong there, he stood at the window barking, lifting both front feet off the floor at once. Or, he would perform a fair imitation of a Lipizzaner stallion in the way he shook his head and pranced, lifting each leg high and one at a time, but never moving forward or back. Move over, Michael Jackson! Jaw-dropping moves for any dog, let alone a large, aging Belgian Shepherd.

Hero was born in South Carolina and had been owned by a soldier who trained him well, as evidenced by Hero's responsiveness to commands when Paul adopted him. The man was deployed overseas where he was killed in the line of duty. He had left Hero with his parents who could no longer keep him after receiving news of their son's death. They placed Hero in a shelter where he remained for two years because the shelter would not allow him to be adopted out. With his unique dance, the shelter used him in commercials and fundraisers, a "poster" dog, until a rescue organization succeeded in freeing Hero. The organization began an immediate search for Hero's forever home.

As it happened, Paul was looking to adopt a dog having lost his last Shepherd, Taj, some months earlier. The rescue people brought two Shepherds to Paul's house. The first dog out of the vehicle displayed aggressive behavior toward a toy. Paul asked to see the other dog. He and the then three-year old Hero bonded on sight.

DOUBLE THE "FUN"

My first assignment with Sassy and Hero together began without drama. Hero regarded me with a watchful calm from the living room sofa. Sassy remained in close proximity to Hero and didn't bark much until I took Hero for his walks, at which time she barked nonstop until we returned. I could hear her high-pitched bark from half a block away when the windows were open.

Dana and Paul's bed on which I slept presented a daunting prospect requiring either a step stool or a springboard to clear the mattress. Granted, I stand a mere 5'1" (in heels), but when I positioned myself next to the mattress, it reached almost to my shoulders. There was no graceful ladylike way to get into bed. I adopted the habit of running up to it, reaching as far across the bed as I could, throwing one leg up, grabbing a piece of sheet and kind of pulling myself up the rest of the way. No way could Sassy make that leap, so she slept on the floor beside the bed. Hero had a bed on the other side.

In true Shepherd fashion, Hero chose to remain downstairs at night to guard his domain or perhaps to wait for Paul's return. The consequences of Hero deciding to sleep downstairs made for a difficult first night. Sassy remained with him but found herself in a canine Catch22: She wanted to sleep in her own bed upstairs but was unsure about sleeping up there with me. So, she acted out as any indecisive neurotic small dog (or large dog) would in a no-win situation. She vocalized her frustration by barking much as she had the first night I had spent with her in her own house, which did nothing to foster positive feelings on my part toward the little girl.

Talk about déjà vu! After several hours of attempted sleep, I tried to lure Sassy upstairs, but Hero was on the sofa next to where Sassy lay on the floor and growled softly as I approached Sassy. Hero, a gentle dog by nature, was protective of Sassy and may have seen me as a threat to her. Since I wasn't about to test Hero's gentleness against his protective instinct, there was nothing for me to do but return upstairs and resign myself to a sleepless night. But I think that after my initial trip downstairs, Hero may have admonished Sassy in doggie speak to be quiet and stop being a brat because I heard not another sound from her.

Sassy and I continued a tense relationship through the following morning until one time when I needed to use the bathroom. I sat on the john doing my thing, and Sassy came running in smiling, tail wagging and stood up on her hind legs with her front paws against my knees. For the first time since I'd known her, she allowed me to pet her head and scratch behind her ears.

Our relationship progressed from that point on, although any attempt at affection toward her had to be on her terms. If I approached her and attempted to pet her, she would either run away or snap at me and then run away. The only times I could bet on being allowed to touch her were when I was in the bathroom. I didn't have a private pee again for the entire week. But she did sleep on her bed next to me, and she curled up as close to me as she could get when I watched television from the sofa downstairs. While Sassy no longer exhibited a visceral fear of me and ventured out of Hero's shadow more often to follow me around the house, Sassy was still Sassy and would sometimes snarl at me for no apparent reason.

And then I undid all the progress I'd made with her when I carried a bowl of hot soup into the den to eat while I watched *The Young and the Restless* and tripped over a dumbbell that hadn't been pushed back against the wall. A good bit of the soup spilled onto the hapless Sassy who had chosen to be underfoot at the time. The poor creature yelped in pain, but there was nothing I could do for her. I couldn't pick her up to comfort her or check the extent of any burns, but I could see reddened skin through her thin white hair where the soup had spilled on her.

Concerned about the severity of possible injury she may have suffered, I walked next door to the neighbor whom Dana had given as an emergency contact. I told Allen what had happened, adding that Sassy wouldn't come near me since the incident. He offered to bring his two Huskies over to the house and attempt to coax Sassy out onto the deck with them. Sounded like a plan to me.

Hero came out as soon as he saw his two girlfriends, Domino and Bonbon, on the deck. Sassy, not wanting to be left alone, stood in the doorway from where she eyed me with uncertainty. I moved as far away from her as possible, and she crept from the door onto the deck while keeping her distance from Allen and me. I was relieved to see that her burns didn't appear as severe in the sunlight, and Allen assured me that it didn't look like any serious damage had been done. Sassy must have spent the rest of the day mulling things over and concluded that I could not be blamed for tripping over the dumbbell and spilling the soup on her. It was an accident, and I was a clumsy oaf. All was forgiven as happens so often with animals.

Maybe Sassy began to remember me from one year to the next. Maybe she felt safe enough to approach me with Hero around. Maybe she just mellowed with age. Whatever the reason, after three years she sometimes gave me kisses, allowed me to pet her, and shadowed me almost always. During one visit in particular, much to my surprise and delight, she demonstrated uncharacteristic affection toward me. We were playing on the floor, and she snuggled up to me. I took a chance and reached under her belly expecting her to snap at me. But she let me pick her up, squirming a little until I held her close. I treasured that minute of closeness with Sassy while it lasted. A second opportunity to bond with her to that extent never presented itself.

ANGELS ON EARTH

There come those times when one is reminded to never take for granted or underestimate the love and support of a friend.

Once when I prepared for an assignment with Hero and Sassy, I'd felt nauseated all day despite having nothing in my stomach. The summer heat and humidity may have contributed to my queasiness since Vinny and I had not yet installed a large air conditioner in the house. As the feelings of nausea continued, anxiety stirred within me and increased to the point where I sensed the beginnings of a panic attack.

I felt sick enough by early evening as I drove to Dana and Paul's house that as soon as I arrived, I murmured a weak "hello" and asked if I could go to bed. The windows were open in the house and the central air was not on, and both conditions intensified my feelings of nausea. We had arranged that I would sleep in their son's room, and Danny would sleep on the sofa because they would be leaving for Tahoe at the crack of dawn next morning. After Danny and Paul helped me carry my luggage upstairs, Danny took the time to show me where all the light switches were and how to turn on the big fan in his room. Praise the Lord for that fan!

I felt not a whole lot better next morning as every movement still made me feel rocky, and I'm pretty sure Hero knew I felt sick. Most days, he set the pace at a brisk trot during his early morning walk. But that day, he walked as if he knew every step I took rolled my stomach and increased my feeling of nausea. When we returned from our walk, I fed the dogs, crawled up the stairs, and climbed onto Dana and Paul's bed where I lay with my eyes closed feeling overwhelmed by the idea of moving, even to do something as simple as getting up for a glass of water. The thought of any kind of food caused my stomach to heave, despite having no food in it. My anxiety continued to mount. Convinced I had a brain tumor. Thought I was going to die.

Feeling alone and scared, I wanted someone to be with me. Vinny was working and, in fact, had no idea how sick I felt. I'm a private person and don't broadcast over social media every moment of my day, every time I take a shower, or every time I feel the slightest discomfort. It testifies to my anxiety level that I felt forced to request prayers on my behalf over Facebook. In a private message to those individuals whom I consider friends in real life, and not just fillers for my friends list and vice versa, I posted a plea for prayer that God might relieve my nausea and, by extension, my anxiety. I was touched by the number of people who responded with encouraging and sympathetic words.

My friend Joyce who suffers from chronic pain herself, offered to come by early that afternoon and stay with me for the night. Blessed relief! But she told me she would need to leave me for a few hours to visit her parents who lived nearby and would return to me as soon as she could. I told her I would leave the front door unlocked because Hero might go ballistic if he heard the doorbell. And since he'd never met Joyce…

Hero must have sensed that Joyce was there to help, because he made no objection when she arrived and entered the house bearing saltines and applesauce. Just seeing Joyce made me feel better, and the saltines, a nibble at a time, tasted like manna from Heaven and settled my stomach after a few bites. But the thought of having to move even the slightest bit still rocked me. I know I was poor company while Joyce stayed with me, but she prayed for me and ministered to me with a patience and compassion that could only have come from a God-filled spirit.

Before she left for her parents' house, Joyce took Hero out to the front lawn for a bathroom break. I may have napped a bit while Joyce visited her folks because it seemed like she'd been gone only a few minutes before she returned. I ate a few more saltines and some applesauce. Joyce thinks we watched some of Wimbledon from the bed. Makes sense. I felt better, and I love tennis, especially the Wimbledon tournament for which I would suppress my fear of flying over the Atlantic if I could score tickets to the Men's Final.

Before Joyce went to sleep that night in Danny's room, she again took Hero out. I slept well and awoke the next morning feeling much better—well enough to walk Hero at a close-to-normal pace. Joyce left later that morning with a promise to return if I needed anything.

To this day, I remember with insurmountable love and gratitude how Joyce was there for me in my hour of need giving of her time, her spirit and her heart.

REALITY CHECK

I had a terrifying experience in 2016 which forced me to recognize that the now almost deaf thirteen-year-old Sassy had indeed reached her golden years. One morning on our way downstairs to breakfast, she either misjudged or didn't see the first step, leapt off the landing (something I'd never seen her do before), and tumbled down the full flight in limp rag doll fashion. She yelped once, and a silent scream issued from my open mouth as she reached the bottom and slid on her side across the tiled floor in the entrance foyer. My horror turned to amazement and relief when, before I'd gotten halfway down the carpeted stairs to be with her and check her out, Sassy stood up and raced into the kitchen, uninjured by her fall. Thank you, God, for your mercies, even toward animals.

Besides slowing down as we all do, the elderly Sassy showed her age in another area. She had used newspapers for her toilet in the past, but this practice had deteriorated to the point where she would attempt to pee on them but usually miss, creating a situation that required me to grab paper towels and disinfectant every time I heard the rustle of newspapers. And more to my chagrin, she now pooped wherever she happened to be when the urge came upon her. My custom of walking around barefoot in the house went the way of the dinosaurs, and I got into the habit of watching where I stepped. It was pretty disgusting, but it was also sad to watch as the little girl succumbed to age and physical deterioration.

IN COMMUNICADO

I enjoyed those times when Dana and Paul went away by themselves and left me to sit for Hero without Sassy. His menacing, deep-throated growl could be heard throughout the house, even when he was in the living room and I was upstairs in the bedroom. It was a scary sound, but I knew I never had to worry about prowlers with Hero around. Ghosts, either.

He continued to spend the nights downstairs rather than on his bed next to me. But one night, some nearby sound or movement awakened me from a deep sleep. I looked over with half-closed eyes and saw Hero's massive head inches from my face. Woke me up in a hurry. Turns out he had come to tell me he needed a potty break. Good boy!

I thought it interesting that, one time, he walked away from his food dish to guard the house against the trash collectors outside the house. It seems his instinct to protect trumped his survival instinct.

During one autumn gig with Hero, my general ignorance of all things technical or electronic or otherwise more complicated than a television remote became apparent, making yet another case for the possibility that the final frontier exists between my ears. Hero's house is Belkin wired—lots of hi-tech thermostat-type gadgets that control everything from in-house security cameras to temperature-controlled floors.

It was COLD, about thirty degrees colder than it had been the same time a couple of days before, and this intrepid pet sitter having blood the viscosity of watered-down Kool-Aid running through her veins decided to turn on some heat—just the downstairs heat, and just through the thermostat in the living room that offered what seemed like a gazillion choices. I didn't want to mess with any more of those doohickeys than necessary so nothing too strenuous or elaborate. And it was all good. A few hours later the house was warm, and I turned the same thermostat to "Off." *Oops!* I realized, following several failed attempts to get online, that I'd managed somehow to turn off the central WiFi as well. I returned to the living room thermostat, but no matter how I spun the dial or how many times I pressed the center face on the thermostat, I could not reboot the Internet.

I then started tinkering with some of the other thermostats in hopes of finding some hint as to what might have happened. Nothing! Two hours later and after countless laps around the house, up and down the stairs, I'd lost track of which thermostats I'd "adjusted" and collapsed on a sofa in the den from exhaustion.

I sent text messages to everyone I could think of and, *poof!* WiFi reconnected, and I realized that all my gyrations and anxiety over the past few hours had been for naught. The Internet had crashed of its own volition, had nothing to do with my less-than-minimal technical know-how, and required no assistance to reboot from the bionic multi-tasking thermostats.

As an aside, I watch very little news; it's too depressing, too violent, too biased. It's just too. But I felt a kind of alienation during those few hours when shut out from the Internet. And it occurred to me that it's one thing to choose to stick your head in the sand to hide from unpleasant reality, but it's another to have a bully bury you in it.

RAINBOW BRIDGE

The last time I cared for Hero alone, in April 2017, I noticed several of his tumors appeared to have grown and more had developed although he seemed to be in no apparent discomfort. Dana told me they'd taken him to the vet who advised, "If he were my dog, I would do nothing." Hero was too old to withstand surgery and didn't appear to be suffering.

While Paul and Dana were away that April, Hero didn't always finish his food at one sitting but would eat it at some point before his next meal. I noticed, too, that he ate a lot of grass and produced looser-than-normal stool. Hero's personality remained unchanged. He remained the sweetest of dogs. And he still barked and "danced" when the UPS truck or the garbage truck came up the road.

When Vinny came to visit me and to meet Hero for the first time, Hero wrapped himself between and around Vinny's legs, feline style, something I'd never seen him do. Always aloof for a few minutes with someone he'd never met, Hero took to Vinny at once.

I mentioned all this to Paul when he and Dana returned home. Paul's response despite what he might have felt inside was light, reiterating that Hero was getting old and his body had developed some "quirks."

A week later, I received an email from Ann saying Paul and Dana had put Hero to sleep. His body had been riddled with cancer, and he had stopped eating altogether. I was in tears.

MURPHY'S LAW

Soon after Hero had been put down, Ann reached out to me asking if I'd mind caring for her Sassy while she went to Tahoe in the summer for her family vacation. Three years had come and gone since I'd been to her house. The idea of returning to the scene of the luggage-punctured bedroom wall triggered instant feelings of embarrassment and self-doubt. But a dodger of conflict to the end, I accepted the assignment.

We met for a refresher course in Sassy care a few days before Ann was to leave. She had forewarned me that Sassy had grown "very old" since the year I last saw her when she'd fallen down the stairs. She didn't bark anymore (really?!) and slept all day except for when she needed to eat or relieve herself. While she sometimes used the newspapers, it was not uncommon to find poop and sometimes pee around the rest of the house, especially first thing in the morning. Sassy had lost her sight, as well as most of her hearing. Despite Ann's grim description of Sassy, I was unprepared for the sad-looking little girl who shuffled out from the bedroom where she spent most of every day sleeping on a quilt at the foot of the bed. Sassy's once-wavy hair lay almost lank against her emaciated body, and her head and tail drooped as she stopped short, afraid, when she caught the unfamiliar scent of my presence.

I empathized with Ann's agony as she wrestled with the inevitable heartbreaking decision almost every pet owner must confront when their beloved animal becomes too sick to justify keeping him or her alive. Sassy would be fifteen years old on her next birthday, and her quality of life was far from optimal. But as Ann said, she didn't appear to be sick or in any kind of distress. Her appetite remained good. And Sassy continued to express happiness whenever Ann returned home after being away for a few hours by greeting her at the door with a wagging tail. Ann did everything she could to make Sassy's life as easy and comfortable as possible, including keeping all the doors closed in the bedroom wing except for the one in which Sassy slept to prevent her from walking into the wrong room and becoming confused or frightened. She left lights on for Sassy at night. And she asked that I give treats often to Sassy. It was "one of the few joys Sassy got out of life these days." Poor baby.

The assignment with Sassy began July 4, 2017, and circumstances unfolded almost at once that convinced me I might be in for a rough week. I entered the house and saw with dismay several poops and pees in the hall and in the bedroom where Sassy slept. My stomach lurched. I cleaned the floor and carpet, unpacked my bags, and checked on the sleeping Sassy. With everything under control, I opened the folder left for me by Ann expecting to find some last-minute notes, a set of keys, a check, and her WiFi information. All were included except the last. My funky bad mood after spending half an hour on my hands and knees cleaning up after Sassy slipped another notch downward. I went to the computer for a Facebook fix in hopes of reading at least one uplifting post that would improve my mindset before texting Ann for her WiFi password. But where there should have been a computer, I saw only a keyboard and monitor. I felt the beginnings of an angry panic stir within me as I contemplated having no communication with the outside world and no opportunity to work on my book for two full weeks. In addition, Ann had told me that she and her husband were NOT television people and had only basic cable, which included no premium channels. The daunting prospect of having to endure fifteen days without WiFi, without a computer, and with only mindless commercial-packed drivel on television to fill long empty hours gnawed at me like a starving rat. And as the very real weight of feeling trapped with no hope of escape took its toll, I felt myself morphing into Nicholson's Torrance-esque mentality from *The Shining*. I wanted to flee. I wanted to call Ann and tell her to come home. I could not/would not spend two weeks doing nothing more than playing nursemaid to a dog. Boredom would drive me mad as the immortal and would-be prophetic words of Napolean XIV's, "They're Coming to Take Me Away" partied with discordant fervor in my head. Such was the depth of my frustration.

I telephoned Vinny who, after listening to me spew venom for several minutes, suggested that the monitor might be built into the computer—one of those self-contained things. I'd never heard of such computers, but when I checked the sides of the monitor, I saw all sorts of ports and buttons on the sides. I still didn't see a way to turn it on. Vinny asked for the model number of the computer so he could fish around for an online instruction manual. Turned out all I had to do was push one of said buttons, and I was good to go. Nothing like the obvious to hit home the fact that I needed to move beyond the twentieth century in terms of computer technology. My shoulder muscles relaxed, and the vision of Johnny axing his way through a door receded into the dark from whence it had come.

So my initial text to Ann, rather than containing the language of a woman gone berserk, politely but urgently requested her WiFi information. While I waited for her reply, conditions on the home front deteriorated further. Sassy produced more mess in the hallway and at one point, I slipped on the hardwood floor in pee I hadn't seen. Ann

texted her WiFi info to me later in the afternoon, which helped me-
diate some of the misgivings I felt for having accepted the assignment
with Sassy.

As I relaxed into the Wimbledon tournament and began to think
everything would be okay, yet another shoe dropped when I took a
bathroom break: a large, live centipede in the bathtub! I remembered
seeing several cans of insecticide in the garage, which somehow failed
to alert me as to the possible presence of bugs in the house. So, pray-
ing that the thing in the tub remained where it was, I ran downstairs
(closing the door behind me so Sassy couldn't misstep and fall) for
some anti-centipede spray. The centipede had not moved by the time
I returned to the bathroom, and I exhaled with relief and shuddered
with revulsion as I dispatched it to its final reward. The carcass would
have to remain where it was until Vinny could remove it the first time
he came to visit me. Until then, I would just avoid looking in the tub
every time I went into the bathroom. Thank goodness for a beautiful
and separate shower stall!

The first day wore on, and I realized with a cold shiver that Sassy
made no sound as she picked her way along the hardwood and tiled
floors. She navigated by hugging the walls and large pieces of furniture. I found myself always cautious when rounding corners, expecting to see Sassy standing there watching me with sightless black eyes.
Those deadened eyes, once so full of fun and mischief both saddened
and unnerved me. More than once, I found myself missing what-
I-used-to-consider-her-annoying barking and manic racing around.
Sometimes, out of the corner of my eye, I'd see her pass behind me—
like a silent ghost. The only times I had an inkling of where she might
be were when I heard a thud if she'd walked into something—the
wall, the washing machine, a piece of furniture—or a crash if she'd
knocked something over. The ambience created by being alone, but
not alone, in the large house with one quasi-phantasmagorical dog
and an untold number of very real centipedes drove me into a state
of constant vigilance.

A huge positive in the otherwise oppressive scenario was that Sassy slept most of the day to the extent that I made special trips to the far end of the house just to check on her. She looked miniscule on the puffy folded-over quilt, and she slept with half her body draped so far off the edge that there were times I had to look hard to be sure she was still breathing.

By the second day of having my adrenaline levels redline while on the lookout for Sassy, I hatched a plan for staging a preemptive attack against her accidents by strewing newspapers along the entire length of the house. Success on two fronts! I could now hear rustling papers as she approached so I wasn't startled as often by her presence, and I could clean up after her with minimal effort. But credit where credit is due—she did often use the newspapers strewn about in the laundry room.

After the first week, a routine of sorts took shape. I cleaned up after Sassy, filled her water and food bowls, spent the mornings composing text for my book, cleaned up after Sassy, watched Wimbledon in the afternoons, cleaned up after Sassy, filled her water and food bowls. Sassy's fear of me downgraded to cautious curiosity. Rather than avoiding me when she could, she now stood in doorways facing me with her unseeing eyes. I could almost hear her brain working as she wondered if I were a good witch or a bad witch.

I tried to follow Ann's directive to give Sassy lots of treats, but Sassy would have none of it. She wouldn't accept one from my hand even when I held the biscuit right in front of her nose as Ann suggested, and she refused one that I'd placed in her bowl. I wanted to love her, but Sassy had no intention whatsoever of making anything more than a casual acquaintance of me. I was a mere substitute human who fed her and cleaned up after her until Mommy returned. No love, gratitude, or hint of acceptance would she extend to me. Any bridges we'd built towards each other in the past no longer existed. *Sigh.*

Sassy had also taken to "hiding" in the space between the dining room breakfront and the wall. She'd stick her head in the space and just stand there, sometimes for several minutes. I thought the behavior odd but then wondered if her unhappiness might be so acute—maybe even to the point of depression—from missing Ann that she sought some kind of escape. It broke my heart to think Sassy so miserable and to be helpless to do anything for her.

The second week began, and I awoke to torrential rain. I lay in bed taking in deep breaths for the first time since being at the house, and I allowed the pluviophile in me to luxuriate in the sight and sound of the pouring rain. Sweet peace! Even the sight of Sassy's expected mess in the hallway could not shatter the calm and/or deplete the surge of positive energy I embraced through the sound of rain on the roof and against the windows. Nor could it detract from the brilliant greenness of the rain-soaked grass and leaves—one of my favorite sights.

Energized, I dressed for a workout at the gym looking forward more to the five-minute drive in the rain than to the actual workout. But as I entered the garage from the basement, the universe roared with laughter. The garage floor was wet from a substantial spout of water that projected from the inside cinderblock wall, as opposed to running down the wall like a normal leak. Storage boxes, along with miscellaneous trinkets, papers, and clothes were drenched. So much wreckage! My mind struggled to function as I absorbed the scene, but the prevailing image was that of dampness, lots of dampness. Even as I ticked off ideas of whom I should call first, images of cave crickets, centipedes, and scary creatures galore that love dampness prevailed. I moved a table piled with papers out of the way of the gushing water and dried as much of the rain-soaked stuff as I could. I found a bucket and placed it under the leak, which slowed and stopped as the rain abated.

I called Dana who hadn't left for Tahoe yet. Didn't want to call Ann in California if I could avoid it as there was nothing she could do anyway. After explaining the situation to Dana, she called Ann herself who messaged me stating that the contractor who had been repairing the front steps before she left would stop by to check on the leak.

It probably resulted from something they had done. The contractor showed up two days later. Fortunately, it didn't rain in the interim.

Because this job kept getting better and better, I wondered what else could happen. Not that I had a burning desire to find out, but the answer presented itself a couple of days later. After eating lamb chops one night for dinner, I awoke the next morning with a case of food poisoning that knocked me out of commission for the entire day. I felt miserable, thanked God that I did not have to walk Sassy, and remembered that when I'd thawed the chops the day before, I'd noticed the plastic wrapping had been torn. In fact, I'd known it had been torn for months but chose not to worry about it. My guess is that even though frozen, bacteria had grown on the meat, and to increase the chances of my getting sick, I had eaten the chops rare. Had I paid attention in any of my high school science classes, I'd have known that cold temperatures neither kill bacteria nor prevent them from growing.

The rest of my time with Sassy passed without incident, but I couldn't wait to leave before yet one more disaster occurred. Ann was due home around 9:00 in the morning, so I had cleaned the house, run the dishwasher, and done most of the laundry the previous night. The morning I was to leave, I tossed the bed linens in the washing machine, fed Sassy, laid clean newspaper for her in the laundry room, said goodbye to her, loaded my car, and bailed. I couldn't remember ever having felt so happy and relieved to finish an assignment in my five years of pet sitting.

A few days later, Ann sent a message to me saying she had taken Sassy to the vet to have her put to sleep. Her little body had been wracked with cancer and arthritis. It was time. My heart went out to Ann as I knew how much she'd loved her Sassy. I hope she took comfort from believing that Sassy and Hero were reunited, young and healthy, at Rainbow Bridge.

Thirty-one

Age takes its toll on us humans, too, even on those of us who insist on believing the eternal fantasy that we will never get old so long as we think young. But to nature's inevitable end, my left knee and leg had begun to act up, progressing from an annoying ache when I ascended or descended stairs to a sharp pain when I attempted to rise from a crouched or sitting position on the floor. When I could no longer tolerate the incapacity to dance, ride a horse, or even walk without pain, I received a prescription from an orthopedic surgeon for an MRI. Result: two torn menisci. Really? How'd that happen? I hadn't injured myself. The doc responded with those dreaded words, "It happens when people reach your age. Probably just degenerative." Well! The impact of that declaration hit me like I would imagine a punch to the gut by a prize fighter might. Refusing to release my "eternal fantasy" of being forever young, I scheduled arthroscopic surgery between pet-sitting assignments to make my body "whole and young" again.

Two weeks before surgery in March 2017, I was slated to care for the Montville critters again. The two cats, Gene and Fred, ask nothing more of me than a clean litter box, some breakfast, a few treats, and cuddle time during the evening. The two canine fur babies, Buddy and Keno, require only a morning walk, an hour or so of playtime at the dog park later in the day with their friends, and a couple of potty breaks in the backyard. All the animals reciprocate my attention with love as only animals can. The fifteen-day assignment went off without a hitch.

I had scheduled my surgery for the afternoon Debbie and Phil would be returning home. But the universe has a twisted sense of humor and delights in tossing monkey wrenches into our best-laid plans. It snowed the entire day and into the early evening the night before I was to leave and Debbie and Phil were to return home. This scared me—a lot. Despite owning a four-wheel drive SUV, I am a menace on snow-covered roads, and Buddy and Keno live about twenty miles from my house. I watched the snow fall and worked myself into a lather at the daunting prospect of navigating the roads (and other cars) early next morning. And my clients, who were in contact with me expressed their own concerns about the possibility of a delayed flight into Kennedy Airport. All for naught. The next morning dawned sunny and relatively warm, the plows had done their job while the rest of us slept, and my clients' flight was on time. My drive home, while a nail biter at times because of occasional slushy spots, turned out to be pretty boring.

Vinny drove me to the hospital, and I was in high spirits bopping along to whatever music played on the radio in anticipation of my "fixed" knee. When we arrived at the medical center, I was spooked to learn that I would be under general anesthesia for the surgery. Local anesthesia had been used in previous arthroscopies (fifteen or more years ago). Because I always got sick when recovering from general anesthesia, I requested that something be put in my knock-out cocktail to inhibit my impulse to throw up. "No problem," my anesthesiologist said. "I'm very aggressive when it comes to preventing patients from being sick." So, I was sick for a day and a half following surgery.

After thirty-six hours of post-op misery, I was up and around as I'd expected. My surgeon advised me two days later that I could lose

the over-the-top gigantic icepack they'd given me and no longer needed to keep my knee elevated. And then, he uttered those three most
wonderful words, "Take a shower."

A couple of days later, with the doc's blessing, I embarked upon
a ten-day assignment with Duncan, the Corgi. We walked four times
a day as usual, and played a lot. Two days in, and the symptoms I'd
experienced in my knee before surgery returned along with the additional aggravation of my knee being stiff and sore from the surgical
wound. Great!

I revisited my orthopod when my time with Duncan ended. The
doc insisted that given a little time, all would be well; my knee just
had to heal. According to him, I had overdone it while with Duncan.
Take it easy for a couple of days, he advised. With a resigned sigh, I
retrieved the gargantuan icepack from the closet and returned to bed-
rest with my leg elevated. Once again, Vinny assumed the role of waiting on me hand and foot.

A month later, I returned to Duncan for another ten days. My
knee appeared to be healing and, much to my delight, I discovered
that Duncan had made great improvement in his leash manners. He
now required a slack short leash, at least when there were no distractions, i.e., another person, a dog, a leaf. All bets were off if a squirrel
bounded into his line of sight. To reward him and for the fun of it,
after we'd walked the neighborhood and turned for home, I always
lengthened his leash and jogged; Duncan took off running. He looked
so happy and cute with his short legs working like eggbeaters and his
ears blowing straight back.

In the middle of one such cardio session while running full tilt,
Duncan stopped short to investigate some new smell in the street,
and I, unable to stop as he did, tripped over him and fell flat on the
ground. I mean flat. A quick glance around assured me that my swan
dive onto the pavement had gone unnoticed. *Whew!* I didn't hit my
head or face, and I didn't even skin my knees, just scraped one of my
palms. I think Duncan may have broken my fall. It happened so fast.

We both stood up and shook it off, neither of us the worse for wear. I remember thinking with a smile, not bad for a one-year old puppy and a sixty-six-year old klutz.

First thing next morning, I noticed the pain in my knee had escalated from a dull ache to excruciating pain. And to my chagrin, I discovered that I could no longer hop on my left foot. The circumstances under which I made this discovery escape me. Even worse, my knee stopped working altogether if I remained in one position too long—like more than a minute—rendering me incapable of walking for the first couple of steps. Yet another reminder from those in charge of body deterioration that my particular body might not be as young as I insisted upon deluding myself. I revisited my orthopod who, this time, ordered an X-ray to ascertain the presence or absence of a fracture. No fracture. Doc palpated my knee, moved my lower leg around, and repeated his assurance that nothing was wrong. If I had torn any ligaments, he would have been able to move my lower leg to the side, independent of my thigh. No swelling. No pain upon finger pressure. Take two Advil or other anti-inflammatory medicine three times a day, and if I noticed no improvement in a week, he would schedule another MRI. Okay.

Another assignment with Mia and Milano the following week. I had been feeling guilty about avoiding the gym for several weeks. So, I went. So, I felt much better. And I discovered upon returning to my charges and requesting Alexa to play some rock and roll that I could dance with minimal pain. And, golly gee! My ability to hop on my left foot had returned!

My jubilation was short-lived as, once again, the pain returned less than a week later. My orthopod then suggested I try physical therapy to reduce swelling and break up any possible scar tissue. I began to feel like the doc was taking shots in the dark in hopes that something would work to prevent my reappearance in his office. But I followed his advice and scheduled some PT time with a local center.

Increased discomfort after the second PT session. No improvement after the third. Enough!

I no longer believed or cared what my orthopod said about everything being okay. My body insisted that something was wrong. I would find another doctor and request a knee replacement. The new doc I located turned out to be a kind of botched-surgery repair specialist. He prescribed an MRI for me and, after reviewing the results, repeated the same old litany: nothing unusual in the results. A little swelling and some arthritis, but nowhere near enough to warrant a new knee. *Damn!* Would I consent to another cortisone injection to see if that would improve things?

I have always hesitated to put anything foreign into my body other than the cornucopia of drugs I take to manage my headaches. Doc assured me that cortisone treatments two or three times a year would have no effect on my questionable bone density. And if the cortisone produced no relief, we could try the gel. Red flags popped up. I'd never heard of the gel, and I shy away from any kind of drug or treatment that hasn't been around a while. Too many commercials warning if you or someone you know has taken such and such a drug and experienced such and such adverse reactions up to and including death, you may be entitled to a substantial cash settlement. No, thank you! Not interested in any experiment that, given time, may spawn those kinds of commercials. But I did accept the cortisone shot which resulted in minimal relief for about a week.

Since I didn't want to try the gel, I continued to struggle with my knee pain and associated limitations, and resigned myself to believing that this was as good as it was going to get. I surrendered my thinking to the strong possibility that I would never ride a horse again or dance with abandon or stand up from the floor leading with my left leg. A form of depression began to develop within me, sapping me of appetite and energy. And for a long time making me not much of a fun person to be around.

Thirty-two

Debbie and Phil (my clients from Montville) were touring Alaska. Because I was unavailable during the first week of the Alaskan junket, someone else went to the house to care for the cats, and I retrieved the dogs from doggie camp at the beginning of the second week. Buddy, as usual, went bananas when we passed the dog park on our way home. His disappointment when we didn't make a left into the park was tangible.

What was to develop into a strange week began at dinnertime the first night home when neither Keno nor Buddy touched their dinner. I mean, they sniffed it and walked away without so much as a taste. This was so far out of character for Keno as to cause me concern. A true dog in his eating habits, Keno always gobbled whatever he found in his bowl, as well as anything else he could scavenge from the floor or the street. Even Buddy, the most finicky of eaters would take a bite or two before beginning to "play" with his food. This time, nothing. But Keno did accept his cheese-wrapped anti-seizure Phenobarbital.

Thinking the dogs sensed something wrong with the wet food mixed in with their kibble, I opened a new package the next morning for breakfast. Keno, thirteen years old, now receives Cosequin with his breakfast for arthritic joints, as well as his Phenobarb with each meal. Debbie suggested I break the Cosequin up and mix it in with Keno's food rather than wrapping it in cheese as I did with other dogs who took the same medicine. Keno again refused his breakfast; Buddy finished his. Even though he hadn't eaten his food, I wanted Keno to take his meds, so I wrapped the Phenobarb and the Cosequin in cheese and offered it to him. No problem. Both dogs accepted a Milk Bone without hesitation and exhibited normal treat-eating behavior; Keno wolfed his down in a couple of bites, and Buddy savored every mouthful.

Then some more out-of-the-ordinary stuff. During our morning walks, Buddy waits until we reach the end of a cornfield about a quarter-mile away before he finds a favorable place to take care of business. Keno almost always pees right away and poops soon after. Not this time. During our first morning walk, Keno also held out until we reached the cornfield before he pooped. Coupled with the departure from his normal eating habits, I found this a little disturbing. In the four years I'd been with these dogs, their eating and potty behaviors had seldom, if ever, deviated from the norm. When at the dog park a few hours later, both dogs pooped and acted like themselves in every sense.

Next morning, Keno again didn't eat until I removed the Cosequin pieces from his bowl, after which he ate most of his breakfast and took the Cosequin in cheese. I made a mental note to always give Keno his Cosequin wrapped in something he liked.

At the park, Buddy had some diarrhea; Keno didn't go at all. The boys seemed fine otherwise. Keno took off like a shot along the fence between the large- and small-dog enclosures when Willy arrived, and Buddy trotted around in typical happy-go-lucky fashion.

The dogs weren't the only ones with GI problems. When we returned from the park, I went into Debbie and Phil's bathroom to look for some Pepto Bismol for myself and saw that one of the dogs had been sick on the bedroom carpet (probably Buddy since Keno had almost nothing in his stomach). The mess must've been there for a while because my efforts to clean it up were unsuccessful. I texted Debbie about the dogs' apparent loss of appetite and their GI irregularities, and wondered if maybe the dogs had picked something up from where they'd been boarded before I'd collected them a couple of days earlier. Debbie suggested I give them some white rice if Buddy's diarrhea persisted.

Both dogs devoured that night's dinner without hesitation and played with each other for the first time since we'd been home. Keno pretty much emptied the toy chest looking to find something that might interest either Buddy or me. And I hoped against hope they'd rounded a corner toward recovery.

The next morning's walk produced normal bathroom business. Both dogs went for their breakfast as soon as I put their bowls on the floor. Buddy cleaned his bowl, and Keno ate most of his food after I'd fed him the cheese-wrapped Cosequin. But Keno leaving any food in his dish was just too off. I left his remaining breakfast in place, and he returned to it an hour later and finished it. I began to think that either the Cosequin acted as an appetite suppressant, or Keno's metabolism was changing with age.

As the week progressed, both dogs reverted to near-normal behavior. Buddy fussed with his food but ate most of it. Keno sometimes left a portion of his own meal but always returned to finish it within a half hour. All seemed good.

Since my arthroscopy four months earlier, I continued to struggle with worsening pain in my left knee. A lot of the same pre-surgery symptoms had returned with a vengeance. It hurt to walk, and I had to ascend and descend stairs one step at a time. The act of standing up from a kneeling or crouched position on the floor, as when I cleaned my ferrets' cage, shot bolts of pain through my knee—easily a twelve on a scale of one to ten. Even the act of getting into and out of my car, a standard-transmission Nissan SUV, had become a deliberate process as I maneuvered my left leg with care in order to twist it no more than necessary. Clutch operation took on the odds of winning at a roulette table as the pain from moving my leg from side to side threatened to lock my knee altogether.

But Buddy and Keno's house came with an elevator, something I'd gawked at in amazement when I first saw it and had always shied away from using due to my fear of becoming trapped in closed-in spaces. I would rather lug groceries up the stairs, deal with the gate that prevented Buddy and Keno from getting downstairs to where the cats lived, and fight my way to the kitchen through upturned sniffing snouts than trust that mechanized contraption.

But this week was one of those times that called for desperate measures in the form of succumbing to the ready elevator (trusty cell phone somewhere on my person at all times). That elevator proved to be a phenomenal blessing indeed, and one for which I felt mighty thankful after I'd ridden in it a half-dozen times or so. Made me wonder why I'd been so afraid of it.

Several brick steps lead from the house down to the sidewalk, and I thought for sure I'd break my neck as the dogs hauled me out the front door for their morning walk. I struggled to match their pace even on the street. And then, the second or third day when returning from our morning walk, my knee buckled down and inward without warning when limping up those steps. I spent the better part of the rest of the day on the sofa feeling sorry for myself with my leg elevated and wrapped in ice packs, of which there were plenty, since Phil had undergone double knee replacement surgery a couple of months earlier. And Phil was doing great. I needed to get the name of his orthopod. He dispensed new knees!

I couldn't wait to present my case for a new knee to my own orthopod who could see me no earlier than the following week. Because the knee still supported me, albeit with pain after collapsing on the steps, I couldn't justify a trip to the ER. But I considered it. Keno and Buddy were sorry for their part in my misery; I know they were. I decided to take advantage of their contrition and bring them down in the elevator with me on short leashes next time we walked so we could exit through the garage instead of having to maneuver the outside steps. Both dogs were model citizens and caused no chaos with Gene and Fred.

The strangeness continued. Later in the week, the garage door began to act funky. It would not remain closed with either the remote or the stationary garage door opener. I cleaned some debris from the electric eye and from the edge of the door, after which the door remained closed. But it groaned and clanked more than usual, and it shuddered around the curved piece of track at the top where the door folds into the garage.

Next morning, I rolled the dice and again took the dogs out through the garage for their morning walk. The door opened with the push of a button and remained closed until we returned. I figured yesterday's glitch had resulted from a piece of dried leaf or other debris blocking part of the electric eye, and had been remedied when I swept the ground and garage floor.

With the broken-faucet caper still fresh in my mind (even though the owners had assured me that the faucet fixture had been ready to go), I practiced uncommon (for me) caution and care, especially when at clients' homes. I was scared to death of breaking another house. The night before Debbie and Phil were due home, I heaved an audible sigh of relief after I'd wiped up the kitchen without shattering any glasses or causing the dishwasher to malfunction and flood the kitchen floor. I'd gotten through two weeks (including the assignment before I picked up Keno and Buddy) with all critters and both houses intact. We were safe! Or so I thought.

I spent the next afternoon, my final hours in Montville, doing laundry, returning the house to the condition it was in prior to my arrival, and loading my truck with my things. Debbie and Phil would be home that night. I gave Fred and Gene their evening treats, laughing as Gene chased each kibble I tossed across the carpet. I fed the dogs, let them out one last time and gave them each a treat before riding the elevator downstairs to my truck in the garage. Love that elevator! I pushed the stationary garage door opener on the wall and maneuvered myself into my truck feeling a little sad as I always did when leaving Montville.

As I backed the car up, I heard a weird little groan that didn't at first register with me. And then I felt resistance, something I couldn't ignore, something impeding the truck's progress. I climbed out to check what was going on and felt nothing short of despair upon seeing that the garage door had failed to open all the way, stopping just high enough so as not be seen through my rearview window. The resistance I'd felt was the bottom of the garage door grazing the hatch of my truck.

As soon as I realized what had happened, I pulled the truck forward to assess all damage—a couple of scrapes on the roof just above the hatch, no dents or gouges on the Nissan, but a dent in the garage door, presumably where my truck had pushed it. My heart sank. Another broken house! I wanted to crawl into a deep hole and let the earth swallow me whole.

Forging onward, I tried the garage door opener again. Several times. Whatever had been going on with the door when it would not remain closed a couple of days earlier had worsened. During my first attempt at clearing the gremlins from the mechanism, a loud bang sounded, and a piece of foam insulation flew out onto the garage floor. Now the door would neither stay closed as it had earlier in the day, nor would it open all the way, stopping about three-quarters of the way up but once or twice rising no more than a foot from the ground. I couldn't even get my truck out of the garage, and Debbie and Phil would be home soon.

In a panic, I called Vinny who told me he'd be right over to see what he could do. While waiting for Vinny, I wondered if I could have begun backing up while the door was still opening, but I dismissed that idea. It takes me (and my injured knee) too long to get into the car. But maybe I had pushed the door off the track when my truck bumped it. I was pretty sure the garage door had had no dents before it came into contact with the Xterra's hatch. Of course, I would make restitution for whatever damage fell under my responsibility and, not for the first time, considered buying pet sitter/house-sitter insurance.

Vinny arrived half an hour later and within minutes, had managed to open the door by unlocking the "limit" and pushing the door up manually so I could remove my truck and get it on the street. That was something. He thought that said limit had somehow been knocked out of whack. Anyway, so long as Vinny stood there and operated the limit, the door would open all the way.

Buddy and Keno, meanwhile, were confused as first Vinny and then I went upstairs for one reason or another. It was after 9:00. We'd been working on the door more than an hour and a half, and it was almost that time when I took the dogs out for their final potty break before going to sleep. By a fortuitous twist of fate, Debbie and Phil had landed at Newark Airport on time but were not allowed to disembark for nearly an hour, maybe longer. A frustrating way to wind up a vacation, but it provided Vinny and me more time to work on the garage door.

One time while Vinny finagled with the controls and the door had again stopped three-quarters of the way open, I noticed a little strip of off-center rubber on the bottom of the garage door. And I, like most people who suffer from some degree of OCD, don't like things off-center. I slid what Vinny later called the "safety edge" into alignment, and the door remained closed. One problem solved, compliments of little ol' me.

Vinny adjusted what he called the "opening port," and the door then opened and closed all the way, banging and clanking like Jacob Marley's ghost. I returned inside to let Keno and Buddy out again. And as I followed Vinny home (after closing the garage door), the old maxim "No good deed goes unpunished" wormed its way into my head. Debbie and Phil had been kind enough to accommodate my request that they leave one of their cars outside so I could shelter my thirteen-year old baby in the garage.

When I contacted Debbie the next morning, she was gracious and said that they, too, had noticed the door getting noisier as it opened and closed. She hoped someone would be out to look at it later in the day and insisted that I shouldn't "fret too much." As it happened, the repairman never returned her call, but Phil worked on the door and had gotten it working.

I checked with Debbie a few weeks later on the status of the garage door, and she assured me that Phil seemed to have fixed it because it was still working. Yet again, I find myself counting my blessings for a pool of forgiving clients.

Thirty-three

Friends hung tough with me while I moaned for months about post-arthroscopic pain and revealed various degrees of darkness in my disposition. I didn't like myself much during that time.

My chiropractor had suggested, even before the problems with my leg, that jumping on a trampoline was one of the best ways to counter the onset of osteoporosis. Because Dr. J is a chiropractor extraordinaire and I trust him without reservation, I bought a trampoline and jumped on it several minutes a couple of times a week to music beating cadence through my earbuds—until the day my leg started bothering me. Brought my home cardio to an abrupt stop for about a year. On a whim one day after surgery and after weeks of cursing the pain in my leg, I went downstairs to Vinny's man cave where my mini trampoline had gathered dust from lack of use. I eyed it with suspicion for a second or two and then tried a couple of hesitant bounces. Felt good. So, I grabbed another gear and engaged in several minutes of enthusiastic but not quite rambunctious jumping. When I stepped off the trampoline, I felt the floor wobble as it always does after a bouncing session, and I noticed that for the rest of the day, I had no pain—zero, zilch, zip—in my knee. I could ascend/descend stairs at a near run. No stiffness after I'd remained in one position for longer than five minutes. Forget limping. I still couldn't lead with my left leg when rising from the floor, but I felt good to go more than I'd felt good to go in several months. My leg ached a little when I woke up next morning, but after a return trip to the trampoline, all better!

I still had occasional days of pain and stiffness when on assignment without access to the trampoline. And I wasn't ready to discount the possible role of the recent cortisone shot in my new-found release from pain. But for the most part, I felt almost one hundred percent better—well enough to dance and ride a horse.

But (and it seems there's always a but), ever the self-saboteur, a few weeks after said cortisone shot, I watched a video of a friend busting some line dancing moves I'd never seen. Tried to practice those moves in the kitchen one afternoon with Dwight Yoakam accompanying me with "Guitars, Cadillacs," but I forgot that rubber-soled slippers don't slide. When everything above my left knee quarter-turned to the left, my left foot remained planted where it was. Stars sparkled before me as pain shot through my leg and dropped me to the floor. So, again, I took to my bed with an icepack, and Vinny reprised his role of caretaker. I prayed for healing in a hurry so I could walk Bear beginning the next day. My prayers were answered, but I wore a spandex knee brace for added support and to remind me that I did indeed need to exercise some caution and common sense.

After my exploits on the kitchen dance floor, I twice turned my knee a certain way that resulted in the same degree of searing pain I felt when dancing with Dwight: once while walking Bear, and the second after I'd returned home and stepped up onto a chair to reach the top of the refrigerator. I don't know what I did either time to cause my leg to scream, but I understand now how an animal can chew off its own leg to be released from the agony of a steel trap.

I could not/would not continue through life fearing every move I made, and I returned to my orthopod who, after a quick examination, informed me, "You've torn your ACL." No surgery required as the ACL is the one ligament in the knee which heals itself if given a chance. To that end, I was handed a hinged brace to wear for eight weeks and prescribed yet another MRI to make sure I'd done no further damage to my knee. The MRI confirmed a minor tear in the ACL leaving plenty of ligament intact. And I had sustained no further injury. *Whew!* I loved the support the brace offered, and the freedom from fear that I would experience blinding pain upon some minute movement. In theory, I could remove the brace in time for Christmas as my knee would be good as new.

I was a good patient and wore the brace under "grody" baggy pants and two-sizes-too-large sweats for a couple of weeks until I noticed my left foot and ankle had swollen to twice their normal size. Returned to my doctor—again—who this time, expressed little concern and advised me that if I wanted to, I could remove the brace unless I was at the gym or engaging in some other strenuous physical activity. The idea of not wearing the brace scared me a little, but the thought of fitting into normal jeans again played to my vanity. A day or two later, I found the nerve to shed the brace and was amazed by how strong my leg felt without it. And a couple of days after that, the swelling had all but disappeared. I had never been so happy to see the faint network of spidery purple veins along the top of my foot.

Some days, I think about my pet-sitting assignments and wonder why I do this kind of work at my age. I don't *really* need the extra money, but it does supplement my social security and pension. And then I realize that I make it possible for my clients to go away knowing their fur babies are in good hands. I relieve pet owners of the stress they might otherwise feel worrying about their animals, and I contribute to them enjoying their time away. And that's a good thing. I don't make anywhere near the money I pulled down during my years at Bell Labs and AT&T, but I realize a tangible, visible, and immediate result from my time and effort. Priceless compensation.

Today, about a year and a half since my knee first became symptomatic, I wear the brace most times when at the gym. I have no problem navigating stairs, jogging with Duncan or roughhousing with Keno. Life is good. And as the New Year begins, I look forward with joy and enthusiasm to further adventures with the amazing furry four-legged creatures with which humankind has been blessed.

CPSIA information can be obtained
at www.ICGtesting.com
Printed in the USA
BVHW041812250522
638135BV00004B/43